i ♥ felt

i ♥ felt

33 eye-popping projects for the inspired knitter

felt

KATHLEEN TAYLOR

PHOTOGRAPHS BY BURCU AVSAR & ZACH DESART

The Taunton Press

The Taunton Press
Inspiration for hands-on living®

The Taunton Press, Inc., 63 South Main Street,
PO Box 5506, Newtown, CT 06470-5506
e-mail: tp@taunton.com

Editor: Erica Sanders-Foege
Copy editor: Betty Christiansen
Indexer: Lynne Lipkind
Jacket/Cover design: L49 Design
Interior design and layout: L49 Design
Illustrator: Christine Erikson
Photographers: Burcu Avsar and Zach DeSart

Library of Congress Cataloging-in-Publication Data
Taylor, Kathleen, 1953-
  I (heart) felt : 33 eye-popping projects for the
inspired knitter / Kathleen Taylor.
    p. cm.
  ISBN 978-1-56158-952-4
  1. Knitting. 2. Felting. 3. Feltwork. I. Title.
II. Title: I felt. III. Title: I heart felt.

TT825.T36 2008
746'.0463--dc22

                    2007032217

Printed in the United States of America
10 9 8 7 6 5 4 3 2 1

The following manufacturers/names appearing
in *I ♥ Felt* are trademarks: Clover®, DecoArt™
Crafter's Acrylic™, Knit Picks®, Knit Picks Andean
Treasure™, Knit Picks Memories™, Knit Picks Merino
Style™, Knit Picks Palette™, Knit Picks Shamrock™,
Knit Picks Sierra™, Knit Picks Sparkles™, Knit Picks
Wool of the Andes™, Knit Picks Wool of the Andes
Bulky™, Knit Picks Wool of the Andes Bulky Hand-
Dyed™, Plasti Dip®, Velcro®

To my three sisters, Sandi, Jacque, and Terri.
Thank you for waiting, so patiently.
It's your turn now.

acknowledgments

My undying gratitude goes to my agent, Stacey Glick, and to my editor, Erica Sanders-Foege, whose suggestions were always spot-on and who good-humoredly waited six months for me to realize that I'd been spelling her name wrong.

I would not survive, much less write, without Ann, Shirley, and Melanie, who stuck with me through the joys and neuroses of writing another book; the amazing women of Knitters, Etc., who cheered me along; and Terry, who once again put up with a house full of wet wool.

contents

using
color 74

exploring
embellishments 118

introduction
FELTING
FABULOUS

I don't know about you, but I'm tired of knitting plain, monochromatic projects for felting.

To be sure, the magical transformation from loose and long to small, soft, and fuzzy is always amazing. But the knitting itself—row after row with the same color yarn and needles the size of broom handles—is so totally boring that I have to admit that, at times, I've actually bought felt instead of knitting it myself.

I *want* felted bags, and slippers, and potholders, and hats, and mittens, and decorations. I love the look and feel of felted items, but knitting is not only my passion, it's my comfort and my refuge. And when the knitting is boring, the results are boring.

What's the cure for all this boredom? Pushing your felting to the extreme. Don't be afraid to knit with finer yarns and smaller needles; to strand novelty yarns with wool yarns for great new textures; to experiment with barely felted cable stitches that keep their definition; to expand the design possibilities with felted Fair Isle and intarsia; and, finally, to finish projects with folk-art touches such as beading, appliqué, and needle-felting. All of these are great ways to jazz up your felting, as you'll see in the following chapters.

After all, it's so important to explore color, texture, and embellishment. Take yourself, and your knitting, beyond boredom to fun and fabulous with the projects in this book.

Just plain have fun.

—Kathleen Taylor

the basics

this chapter is going to feel very YADDA YADDA *to knitters who've been felting for a while,* but hang in there with me & READ ON

Even if you've made dozens of hats, bags, and mittens already, I'll show you some new techniques and tips that I think will help your knitting process. ● And for newbies who have yet to shrink anything on purpose, you'll discover there is more to making knitted felt than *knitting it big* and *tossing it in the washer.* Well, not a lot more, but enough that you'll want to sit down and study a bit before you get out the yarn and needles.

what felt is

As most of us already know, knitted felt—which, if we want to get technical, is *fulled* rather than *felted* because we're working with fibers that are already spun—consists of wool yarn, or yarn made with other animal fibers, knit big and loose and then purposely shrunk to form thick, soft, and fuzzy fabric.

The combination of hot water and soap causes the scales on the individual wool fibers to open up. Agitation makes the open-scale fibers mesh together, and cold water causes the scales to close again, forming a dense fabric.

You can make felt by hand, using soap, water, and unspun wool fleece. You can also make felt by using a barbed needle to enmesh dry fibers. We'll be doing some needlefelting on finished felted projects later in this book.

But most knitters make felt by knitting wool yarn with big needles and running the piece through a regular washing machine set on the hot/cold cycle.

Though different kinds of yarn will felt differently (depending on the brand, wool breed, needle size, individual knitting tension, and sometimes color), you can count on losing roughly 25 percent in width and 40 percent in length on plain knitted pieces after felting. That change is sometimes startling and often amusing. People who are unfamiliar with felting will not believe that a gargantuan unfelted slipper (or purse, or mitten) will eventually fit a normal-size human. But it's that transformation that makes felting knits such a fun and fascinating process.

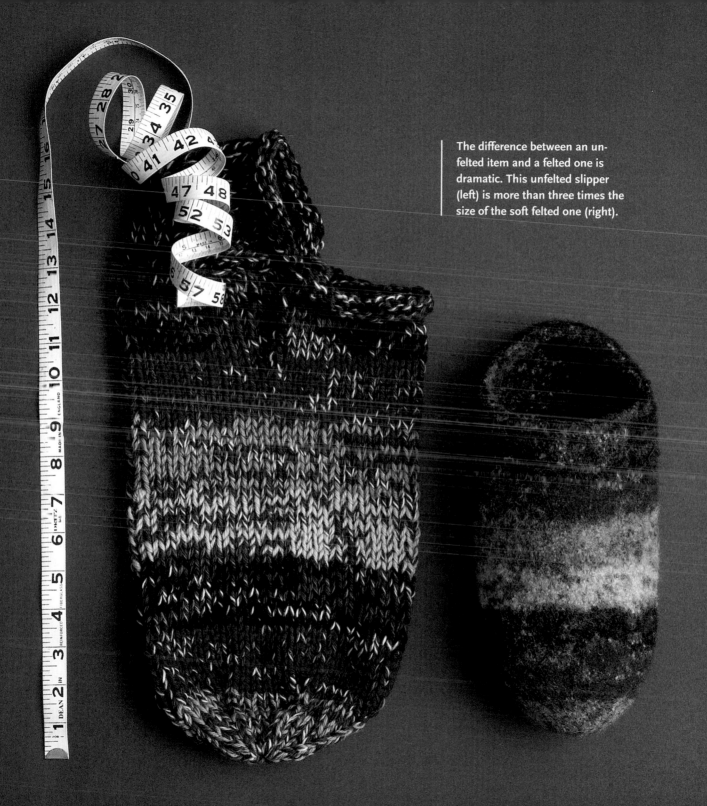

The difference between an un-felted item and a felted one is dramatic. This unfelted slipper (left) is more than three times the size of the soft felted one (right).

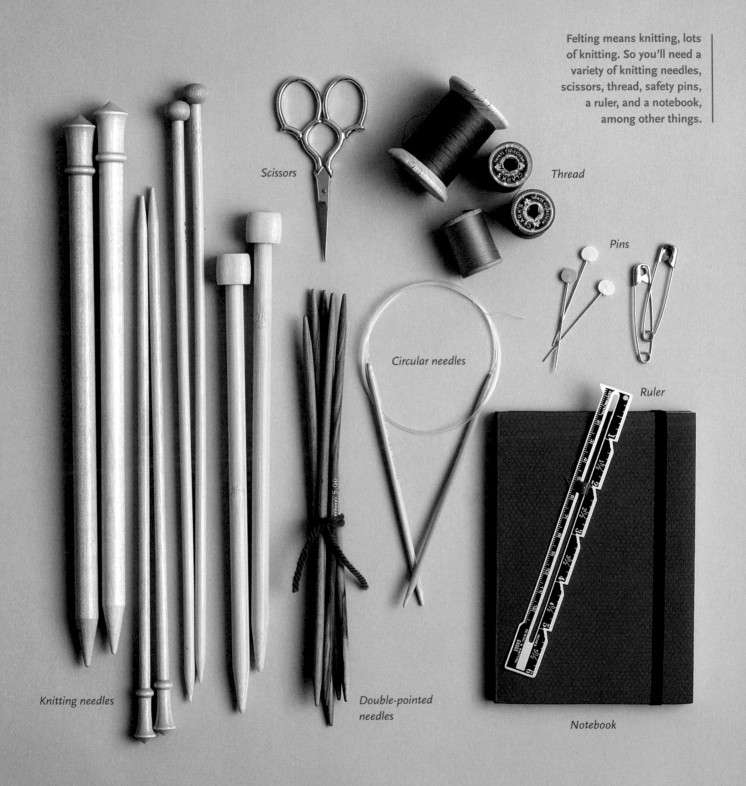

Felting means knitting, lots of knitting. So you'll need a variety of knitting needles, scissors, thread, safety pins, a ruler, and a notebook, among other things.

Scissors

Thread

Pins

Circular needles

Ruler

Knitting needles

Double-pointed needles

Notebook

the most important tool
OTHER THAN YARN AND NEEDLES

Though it is possible to hand-scrub knitted items to make felt, it's a slow, wet, and tedious process. So first and foremost, you're going to need a top-loading washing machine.

I have heard of knitters who felt items successfully in front-loading washers, but because it's not possible to open the door in the middle of a cycle to check the felting progress, your options are severely limited when it comes to making felt. It can be done, but you will be able to felt in full cycles only. That's fine for projects where *fit* is not an issue (ornaments, and most purses and bags). But for clothing items like hats, mittens, and slippers, it is necessary to check the felting progress frequently so pieces can be pulled from the washer when they are the proper size.

Other projects, such as the Alpaca for Her: Cranberry Honeycomb Scarf and the Cabled Evergreen Jacket, are agitated only a few minutes to produce a lightly felted fabric, something that is just not possible with a front-loading washer. But for these projects, you just might want to felt the old-fashioned way— by hand.

needles & notions

Most knitted-felt patterns utilize the larger needle sizes, but several projects in this book use smaller needles as well. You'll want to refer to individual patterns for the exact needle sizes needed for each project, but in general these patterns use straight and double-pointed needles in sizes 8 to 15 (U.S.). Many of the patterns also call for circular needles in various lengths, and in many cases (though not all), circular needles can stand in for straight and double-pointed needles. Since knitting needles are a hefty investment, don't go out and buy all of the sizes until you know which ones you'll need for your chosen projects.

You'll also need a ruler, stitch markers (any sort of ring that fits over your needle will do), safety pins or small stitch holders, large-eye blunt needles, large-eye sharp needles, and whatever notions are called for in each set of directions. If you select any of the cable patterns in this book, you'll also need a cable needle. Jotting notes on yarns used, swatch sizes, and so on in a notebook or journal is also an excellent idea.

For the most part, the notions will be things you might have on hand already: pins, needles, and thread. But you will probably have to purchase additional notions for some of the projects: beads, lining fabric, purse handles, and buttons.

A sewing machine will come in handy for finishing several of these projects.

other non-knitting tools
YOU'LL NEED

This list is pretty short: a mesh zippered lingerie bag and some gloves to protect your hands as you check the felting progress. A pair of tongs to fish the wet lingerie bag out of the washer is nice, but not necessary.

Your mesh lingerie bag needs to have a zipper closure because tied lingerie bags often come untied during the heavy agitation needed to felt knitted pieces.

yarn & fiber selection

Here's the most important thing to remember about yarn: Only animal fibers felt. Cotton will shrink, but it does not felt, and most man-made fibers don't even shrink. In order to make a felted fabric with your knitting, the primary yarn must be spun from predominantly animal fiber: wool, mohair, alpaca, and so on.

Yarn that is a blend of animal fiber and man-made fiber *can* felt if the fiber percentage is around 80 percent animal. You can also strand lightweight novelty yarns spun entirely from man-made fibers (polyester, rayon, nylon) with wool yarn to make interesting textures in the finished fabric, but the man-made fibers should compose no more than 20 percent of the entire piece. In other words, the wool yarn has to be heavier and stronger than the nonwool portion in order for the piece to felt.

To complicate matters, some wool breeds are resistant to felting, including breeds that have a short, wiry, and curly staple, like Suffolk. On the other hand, some wool breeds felt almost instantly, like Merino. Most wools fall somewhere in the middle, and most will felt satisfactorily.

Here's the second most important thing to remember: Even on a wool yarn, check the yarn label. If the words *superwash, machine washable,* or *felt resistant* appear anywhere on the label of the yarn you intend to use as your primary yarn, as obvious as it sounds, you need to select another yarn. Those wool yarns have been specially treated not to felt, which is sorta the opposite of the goal in this book.

Even some theoretically *feltable* yarns will not felt. Some (though not all) white, yellow, and very light-colored yarns have been treated to achieve their pale color. That treatment sometimes interferes with the yarn's ability to felt. Always knit and felt a test swatch when working with white and very pale yarns before beginning a project.

WARNING:
Yarns labeled SUPERWASH, MACHINE WASHABLE, or FELT RESISTANT will not felt. Do not use these yarns as your primary yarn in any felting project.

The third most important thing to remember is this: Felting does not change the fundamental nature of the yarn. If your yarn is scratchy before you felt it, it'll be even scratchier after felting. If your yarn is yummy-soft before felting, it'll be even more yummy-soft afterward. If your yarn is fuzzy before felting, it'll be fuzzier still afterward. (Come to think of it, nearly every felted yarn comes out a little fuzzy, but yarns like brushed mohair increase the final fuzziness exponentially.)

Any weight of wool yarn will felt. Historically, most knitted-felt projects have used either a bulky yarn or several strands of worsted-weight yarns held together for a stiff fabric. These projects use bulky, worsted-weight, and DK-weight yarns for a good variety in finished fabric weight.

swatching:
IT'S MANDATORY

TIP

Most of the yarn requirements in this book have been adjusted to include sufficient yarn for making swatches.

You heard me: Swatching is mandatory. Period.

Even if you use exactly the same yarns and colors recommended in this book, you won't know how your particular washer will handle those yarns. Until you knit and felt a swatch, you won't know if the yarn you selected will actually felt. You won't know how much your yarn will shrink, or how fast. You won't know if your colors will run. You won't know if your colors and/or stitch pattern will look good after felting (short pattern repeats and subtle color changes can disappear entirely as the piece shrinks). You won't know the thickness or texture of the finished fabric until you felt a swatch.

Yes, I know it's a pain. But making and felting swatches is not nearly as painful as knitting a large project only to find that half of the yarn you used doesn't shrink, or that one of the colors bleeds, or that your painstakingly knit Fair Isle pattern is indistinguishable from the background.

And honestly, it doesn't take that long to knit and felt a swatch. Swatches don't have to be huge—for a stockinette-stitch swatch, 20 stitches is sufficient. If your project is a single color, 30 rows will give you enough fabric to measure (before and after felting) and to judge whether that yarn is a good choice. If your project involves stripes or color changes, then knit at least several rows of each color in your swatch, even if the swatch exceeds 30 rows.

If your pattern calls for cable stitches, adjust your stitch number so that you incorporate at least one entire pattern repeat in the width, and several cable repeats in the length of the swatch. You should knit two or three full cable repeats in order to track the vertical shrinkage of your swatch.

If your pattern calls for Fair Isle or intarsia knitting, adjust your stitch number so that you incorporate at least one entire pattern repeat in the width, and each of the colors and design elements in the length. An intarsia swatch need not be an exact image of the finished pattern chart—just make sure that each color is represented in your swatch.

I know this will be hard for conservation-minded knitters, but felt the swatches for each project separately. Some yarns shed a great deal (mohair blends, especially), and the fibers lost from one swatch can become permanently incorporated in any other pieces in the same washer load.

taking note

Before felting your swatch, write down the yarn you're using (color number, manufacturer, fiber content, weight, yards per ball or skein) or, better yet, tape the yarn label to your journal page. Write down your needle size. Write down how many yarn strands you're holding together. Write down the number of stitches and the number of rows in the swatch. If you're working anything other than plain stockinette stitch, write down your stitch pattern. Measure and write down your gauge (stitches per inch and rows per inch). If your gauge differs from the recommended gauge listed in the pattern, adjust your needle size until the gauges match. Measure your swatch with a ruler placed in the middle of the piece and flatten it on a hard surface. Measurements are often given as approximate in the instructions because loosely knitted fabric stretches very easily. Try not to stretch the fabric while measuring it. Write down the total measurements of your swatch: width and length.

After felting (remember to check the swatch several times during the washer cycle to monitor felting speed), write down the new swatch measurements. Note the length of agitation needed to felt the swatch (i.e., several minutes, an entire cycle, more than one washer cycle). Note any unusual shrinkage (if one yarn or color shrinks more or less than other yarns or colors). Note the texture, especially when stranding novelty yarns with plain wool yarn. Note any bleeding, fading, or color change in the piece (some yarn colors mute and soften while felting). Note the thickness of the felted fabric.

Trust me, you won't remember any of that stuff three projects down the line. You'll be very glad to have thorough notes.

If you're not sure what kind of fabric you want for your finished project, knit several swatches, remove each swatch at a different point in the washer cycle, and then measure the shrinkage of each. Compare the swatches and decide how to proceed. If you prefer the thicker fabric of a more heavily felted swatch, adjust the length and width of your project to compensate for additional shrinkage.

If your project is to be knit in the round and cut open afterward (for instance, the Child-Size Gingham Vest on p. 112), you can knit your swatch in the round, and then cut the tube open after felting for final measurements. Once your swatch has been felted, and the yarns/colors/patterns meet your requirements, go ahead and start your project. You don't have to wait for the swatch to dry.

general knitting
FOR FELTING

For the most part, you knit for felting the same way you'd knit anything else: by keeping an even tension on your yarn and working uniformly. When you change colors (either at the beginning of a row/round or when you tie on another ball of yarn for intarsia), always leave at least 3-in. tails on the new and old yarns. Do not weave those ends in, as the extra bulk can distort the felting.

The only time you need to weave in ends is at the cast-on or bind-off row. In those cases, thread the tails in a large-eyed needle, bring the needle through several loops on the wrong side of the work, and trim the excess tails closely.

Before felting the piece, tighten and check all of the knots and trim the tails to 1 in. or less. After felting, trim the knots and felted tails flush with the felted fabric.

felting cabled knits

TIP

Do not overfelt cabled projects. Too much felting will cause the cables to look like fuzzy blobs.

Except for using larger needles, knitting cables for felting is also the same as knitting cables that aren't going to be felted. All of the cable stitches used in this book are explained fully in each pattern, and charts are provided for those projects where a chart is applicable.

Note: The difference between *felted cables* and *felted anything else* is in the size of the finished piece. With cables, the finished, lightly felted piece is often wider, and sometimes longer, than before felting.

TIP

Lightly felted items may still ravel if cut. Finishing a cut edge with either hand- or machine-sewn stitches will prevent raveling.

I know that sounds like it makes no sense, but unfelted knitted cables are very elastic—the cables and ribs draw the fabric in. A quick felting (usually 10 minutes or less) will not only felt the yarn slightly, but it will also relax the cables and stitches, so that the finished felted piece is often wider than the unblocked, unfelted original.

On projects with a fair amount of width and length (the Cabled Evergreen Jacket on p. 68, and the Cabled Tote on p. 64), felting will cause the piece to lose some length, though not a lot. On long, narrow projects (the Alpaca for Her: Cranberry Honeycomb Scarf on p. 58), the item may end up both wider and longer than the original, depending on how the piece is stretched and blocked after felting.

felting fair isle

Knitting Fair Isle for felting is *not* like knitting Fair Isle for nonfelted projects. The stranded floats, which are the unused yarns carried on the wrong side of the fabric in each row, will shrink more than the knitted stitches because the carried yarn strands tighten more than the knitted stitches. This means that felted Fair Isle items will draw in more than pieces knitted in a single color. So *every row* in a felted Fair Isle project, even those worked in a solid color, *must* be stranded, including the cast-on and bind-off rows.

What this means is that in order to ensure even felting of a Fair Isle project, you must cast on stitches using yarn from alternate balls of yarn (following the chart if the cast-on row is a two-color row, or using two balls of the same color if the cast-on row is a single-color row). The same principle applies to the bind-off row. If the

TIP

*You must strand
every row, even
solid-color rows,
in felted Fair
Isle. Cast on and
bind off using
alternate balls of
yarn as well.*

bind-off row is a two-color row, strand the yarn as you bind the stitches off. If the bind-off row is a single color, you must alternate stitches from two balls of the same color yarn in order to ensure that the edges of the piece will felt uniformly.

All of the Fair Isle patterns in this book have accompanying charts and are written for knitting in the round. To follow the chart, begin at the lower right corner of the chart and work across the row from right to left, repeating the pattern as needed. Begin the next round at the next square up on the lower right corner of the chart. Follow the chart, working up the design, one row of squares for each round of knitting. Due to the shrinkage of the floats on the wrong side of felted Fair Isle, those pieces will shrink more than the same number of stitches and rows worked in a single color.

felting intarsia

Felted intarsia pieces are worked nearly the same way unfelted intarsia pieces are knit: New colors are tied on for each color section, the pieces are worked back and forth (rather than in the round), extra yarn can be wound on small bobbins, and new yarn colors must be wrapped around the old colors when making a color change.

The difference in knitting intarsia for felting is that you cannot strand the yarn behind more than two or three stitches in the design because the floats on the back of the work will shrink more than the knitted stitches. It is best to tie on new lengths of yarn, even for small color sections.

Following an intarsia knitting chart is not much different than following a Fair Isle knitting chart, except that intarsia is knitted flat (back and forth), rather than in the round.

finally,
how to felt your knits

TIP

Do not combine pieces from different projects in the same felting batch. Even all-wool felted items shed fibers, and wool/mohair yarns can shed copiously. Those shed fibers can become permanently embedded in your other projects, causing colors to muddy and texture to change.

TIP

All yarns felt differently. All washers felt differently. All knitters have a different notion of when the felting is complete. Be open to experimentation and check the progress of your felting frequently. You decide when the piece is finished.

Okay, you have your finished swatch (because you're knitting swatches before trying a larger project, right?), and you want to felt it. It's easy to do:

1. Place the swatch (or if you have progressed far enough, the finished item) in a small mesh zippered lingerie bag. There are larger mesh bags available for the medium-size projects. Some large projects (like the bigger bags and the Cabled Evergreen Jacket) won't fit into even the largest lingerie bags. Those projects are felted unbagged. Unless the individual instructions specifically state to leave the item out of a bag, always use a lingerie bag.

2. Put the bagged item in your washer. Pour a small amount of laundry soap directly on the item. (I use liquid soap. If you use powder, just sprinkle it on the item.) By "small amount," I mean less than one quarter of the amount you usually use in a full load.

3. Set your washer to the hot wash/cold rinse cycle. Set the load size to small (or medium, if you're felting one of the larger projects).

4. Set the cycle time to the longest allowed by your washer and start it.

5. After about 5 minutes of agitation, open the washer lid, stop the agitation, put gloves on (the water will be very hot), pull the lingerie bag out, and check the

felting progress. If the piece is felted to your satisfaction, replace the bag and spin the washer out (and proceed to step 6). If the piece is not felted to your satisfaction, replace the bag and start agitating again. Check in another 5 minutes. Continue checking the progress until the felting satisfies you, or the wash cycle finishes.

6. If the full wash cycle has run and the piece is not felted to your satisfaction, skip to step 7. If the piece is felted to your satisfaction, and you have spun out the washer, remove the lingerie bag. Take the items out of the bag. Rinse them gently with lukewarm water until the soap is gone. You can return the piece to your washer and spin the excess moisture out, or you can roll the wet piece in a towel to remove the excess water.

7. If the piece has not felted to your satisfaction after a full wash cycle, allow the washer to go into the cold rinse cycle. Check the progress every 5 minutes as before.

8. If the piece has not felted to your satisfaction after an entire washer cycle, repeat the entire washer cycle (checking the progress at 5-minute intervals as before).

9. When the piece is felted to your satisfaction, and the excess moisture is removed (either by spinning or rolling the piece in towels), shape the felted piece. Do not be alarmed if the piece is skewed and crooked. Pull the piece into shape, straightening the edges. If the piece needs additional shaping, form the shape with your hands. You can place the piece on a form to dry or stuff it with plastic bags to hold the shape.

10. Allow the piece to air-dry. It will take about one day for a flat piece to dry. It may take longer for pieces that are on forms, or stuffed with plastic bags, to dry.

11. After running a felting batch, be sure to put your washer back on the normal settings (you don't want to felt anything accidentally). Also, use a paper towel to wipe any leftover fibers out of the tub of your washer so they don't end up in your next batch of laundry.

Troubleshooting:
THAT'S NOT WHAT I THOUGHT IT WOULD LOOK LIKE

You've finished felting your piece and it doesn't look right: Don't panic.

If the piece is too large, run it through another washer cycle and see if that helps. If the piece is too small, soak it in hot water for a few minutes, then pull and stretch it as much as you can. You can often add as much as 15 percent to the length and width of a felted piece just by stretching.

Felt is fabric—if an opening is too tight, cut a bigger opening. Trim the felt carefully, until the opening is the right size.

If an opening is too big, cut a wedge or strip out of the fabric and use matching thread to whipstitch the opening closed. Brush lightly over the seam, and it will be barely visible. Or embroider/bead/appliqué over the seam, and no one will ever know it is there.

Long, narrow pieces (like I-cords and handles) often come out of the washer longer than they were when they went in. That can work in your favor, but if a handle or cord is too long, just trim the excess and sew it back on the piece. Brush over the seam lightly, cover the seam with a button, or embroider/bead/appliqué over the seam, and no one will ever know it is there.

Some thick felted pieces can be creased in the washer's spin cycle. If that happens, steam-press the unwanted crease out before the piece dries completely. If the crease doesn't disappear completely, embroider/bead/appliqué over the crease, and no one will ever know it is there.

If an item simply can't be pulled, cut, or shaped into something that pleases you, don't toss the felt. Cut it up and use the pieces to appliqué on other projects. Or cut it into pieces and make pins and ornaments with embroidery/beading/appliqué.

Be inventive. While designing projects for this book, a slipper prototype came out of the wash looking much more like a small purse than a slipper. So I added a handle, and *voilà*, it turned into a purse.

caring for your felt

Care for your finished pieces as you would any other fine knit item: Hand-wash carefully if necessary (or dry-clean), reshape the item by hand, and allow it to air-dry. Wool and animal fibers are prone to attacks by wool moths, so store your items in airtight bags during the off season. Finally, don't leave your felted items in direct sunlight for long periods of time, because the sun not only can fade the colors, harsh sunlight can weaken the wool fibers.

Now that you've made it through the basics, have a great time exploring the projects in the following chapters. Don't be afraid to make a mistake; wonderful things can come of so-called mistakes. After all, how do you think we came to have such a wonderful thing as felting?

PLAYING WITH texture

who says felted knits have to be **FLAT, HARD & SMOOTH?** *explore the softer side of felting* with the ALPACA FOR HIM: hat & scarf set.

Play with bobbles and raised ridges with **the Big Bag** *and* **Bobble Bucket Hat and Scarf.** *Strand an eyelash yarn with wool for the* **Child-Size Shaggy Slippers** *and the little bag we jokingly tagged* **"It Looks Like a Purse."** *Experiment with lightly felted cables with the* **Alpaca for Her: Cranberry Honeycomb Ear Warmer and Scarf set,** *the* **Cabled Tote,** *and the* **Cabled Evergreen Jacket.**

the big bag

Everyone needs a Big Bag for knitting, or shopping,

or just for fun. This Big Bag has a twist—the raised-rib handles are knitted in the piece with contrasting yarn. Worked with beautiful Noro Iro wool/silk yarn for the body and Cascade 220 Tweed for the handles, your Big Bag can be finished with felted side ties and decorative buttons for a great look. Sew a smaller canvas bag to the inside for a practical pocket.

Yarn:
Noro Iro, 75% wool/25% silk, 100 g, 131 yd., #93 (green/blue/pink/gold/burgundy/peach/brown/black), 5 skeins
Cascade 220 Tweed, 90% Peruvian highland wool/10% Donegal wool, 100 g, 220 yd., #622 (charcoal tweed), 2 skeins

Yarn Weight:
Iro: bulky; 220 Tweed: worsted

Needles:
Size 13 (U.S.) circular, 24 in.; size 10 (U.S.) dpn

Tools:
Large-eye blunt needle
4 yarn bobbins
4 safety pins

1 stitch marker
Sewing needle

Notions:
16½-in. by 6-in. piece of ¼-in. plywood, with corners rounded
Purchased canvas tote bag: 12 in. by 12 in.
1¾-in. Clover® Magnet Tote Bag Closure
4 buttons, 1 in. or larger
Matching sewing thread

Unfelted Gauge:
3 sts = 1 in., 4 rows = 1 in. in stockinette st

Number of Complete Washer Cycles to Felt as Shown:
(Adjust as necessary to achieve desired size.) 2 for bag, 1 for ties

Size before Felting:
25 in. long, 26 in. wide, lying flat; handles 15 in. long, 1¾ in. wide

Size after Felting:
(NOTE: Sizes can vary due to individual washer cycles. Finished items that are too large can be felted again. Finished items that are too small can be stretched while wet to add about 15 percent additional length and/or width.) 16½ in. wide (with bottom shaping done and plywood bottom in place), 12 in. long; handles 11 in. long

Number of Yarn Strands Used:
1 strand Iro; 2 strands 220 Tweed for bag and handles; 1 strand 220 Tweed for ties

KNITTING INSTRUCTIONS

With size 13 circular needle and 1 strand of Iro, CO 148 sts. Make sure the stitches aren't twisted, and join.

RND 1: K. Place stitch marker at end of rnd.

Work even until piece measures 2½ in.

Wind double strands of 220 Tweed on 4 yarn bobbins. Add more yarn to bobbins as needed.

HANDLE RND 1: *K37, tie on 1 220 Tweed bobbin, CO 5 sts with 220 Tweed*, repeat 3 more times.

HANDLE RND 2: *K37 with Iro, pull 220 Tweed to right side of needle and wrap it around Iro, K5 with 220 Tweed, pick up Iro*, repeat around.

Repeat Handle Rnd 2 until piece measures 25 in.

NEXT RND: BO all Iro sts, place each set of 220 Tweed handle sts on a safety pin.

Handles

Place any set of 5 handle sts on size 13 needles. Work sts with 2 strands of 220 Tweed in stockinette st (working back and forth) until handle measures 15 in. BO all sts. Repeat with the other handles.

I-Cord Ties (make 2)

With 1 strand of 220 Tweed and size 10 dpn, CO 3 sts.

ROW 1: K across.

ROW 2: Slide the sts to the right end of the needle. Pull the yarn behind the work to the beginning, K across. Repeat Row 2 until tie is 36 in. long.

LAST ROW: Sl 1 st, K2 tog, PSSO. Cut 6-in. tail, pull tail through loop, and tighten. Weave tail inside the I-cord.

Shaping the Bottom

1. Lay the bag flat with the front and back handles lined up. With 1 strand of Iro threaded in a large-eye blunt needle, sew the bottom of the bag together.

2. Turn the bag inside out. Following the Big Bag Corner Stitching Diagram, with the center bottom seam positioned as shown, measure 6 in. down both sides of the corner and mark. Using 1 strand of Iro threaded in a large-eye blunt needle, stitch across the corner as shown in the diagram. Repeat with the other corner. Turn the bag right side out again.

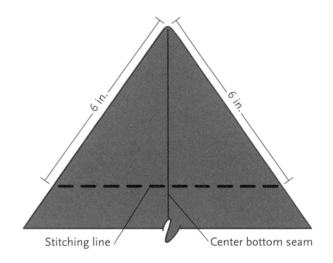

6 in.   6 in.

Stitching line   Center bottom seam

BIG BAG CORNER STITCHING DIAGRAM

FELTING

This bag is too large to fit in a mesh lingerie bag. Place the I-cord ties in a small mesh zippered lingerie bag. Wash the bag and ties on the hot/cold cycle. Check the progress frequently and remove the ties when the desired amount of felting has taken place (probably 1 full cycle). After the first felting cycle is complete, take the bag out of the washer and trim the excess corner fabric. Return the bag to the washer for another complete cycle. Remove and pull the bag into shape, making upper edges straight. Pull on the raised ribs to straighten them. Trim any felted yarn ends flush with the fabric. Hand-shape the bag and set it upright. The handles will curl on their own. You can leave them curled or you can steam-flatten them later, as you wish. Stuff the bag lightly with plastic bags, if desired, to hold the shape. Allow the bag and ties to dry.

ASSEMBLY

1. Trim the handles from the purchased canvas bag and discard them. Place the canvas bag centered between the handles on the back of the bag, 1½ in. down from the upper edge. Using matching sewing thread, stitch the upper edge of the canvas bag to the Big Bag for a pocket.
2. Following the instructions on the package, apply the magnet closure pieces to the center front and back of the bag. Fold the prongs inward if your button is not larger than 1 in. Sew decorative buttons over the magnet closure.

3. Measure and trim the handles to 11 in., if necessary. Overlap the upper edge of the front handles 1¼ in. Using matching thread, stitch the front handles together. Sew a decorative button centered on the overlap. Repeat with the back handles.
4. Measure and mark 1 in. down from the upper edge, every 1³/₄ in. across the sides (between the handles) for the eyelets (6 on each side) Cut a ¼-in. vertical hole at each pin. Beginning on the right side, thread a tie through the 6 holes on one side. Tighten and tie in a bow. Repeat on the other side.
5. Place the plywood piece with the rounded corners in the bottom of the bag for stability.

bobble bucket hat

Texture and color come together in this adorable

bucket hat. Horizontal raised ridges divide colorful bands dotted with contrasting bobbles. Sized for child through adult, this hat knits quickly and felts beautifully.

Yarn:
Cascade 220 Quatro, 100% Peruvian highland wool, 100 g, 220 yd., 1 skein each of #5011 (orange), #5019 (green), #5018 (blue), and #5017 (purple)

Yarn Weight:
Worsted

Needles:
Size 11 (U.S.) dpn, 10 in.

Tools:
Large-eye blunt needle
3 safety pins

Sizes:
Child (Youth/Adult)

Unfelted Gauge:
3.5 sts = 1 in., 4 rnds = 1 in. in stockinette st

Number of Complete Washer Cycles to Felt as Shown:
(Adjust as necessary to achieve desired size.) 2

Sizes before Felting:
Approx 13½ in. (14 in.) long, 12½ in. (13½ in.) wide, lying flat

Sizes after Felting:
(NOTE: Sizes can vary due to individual washer cycles. Finished items that are too large can be felted again. Finished items that are too small can be stretched while wet to add about 15 percent additional length and/or width.) 4¼ in. to crown edge for all sizes, approx 22 in. (24 in.) around

Number of Yarn Strands Used:
1 strand throughout

KNITTING INSTRUCTIONS

With purple and size 11 needles, CO 90 (100) sts. Divide the sts on 3 needles as evenly as possible. Make sure the stitches aren't twisted, and join.

RNDS 1–5: K.

RND 6 (RIDGE RND): With the tip of the left needle, reach inside the work and pick up one CO loop directly below the stitch. Knit those 2 loops together. Repeat around. Cut purple.

RND 7: Tie on orange. K 5 rnds.

BOBBLE RND: See "The Bobble Stitch" on the facing page for bobble instructions. *K9 with orange, work bobble with blue*, repeat around.

Work even for 5 rnds with orange.

Cut orange. Tie on purple. K 5 rnds.

PURPLE RIDGE RND: With the tip of the left needle, reach inside the work and pick up the lowest purple loop directly below the stitch. Knit those 2 loops together. Repeat around. Cut purple.

Repeat the band and bobble sections for all sizes, with a purple ridge in between each, in this order: blue band with green bobbles, green band with orange bobbles. Repeat the orange band with blue bobbles, but do not work the purple ridge.

NEXT RND (YOUTH/ADULT SIZE ONLY): With orange, *K8, K2 tog*, repeat around. (90 sts remain)

NEXT RND AND ALL EVEN DECREASE RNDS, ALL SIZES, UNTIL NOTED: K.

DECREASE RND 1 (ALL SIZES): *K7, K2 tog*, repeat around. (80 sts remain)

DECREASE RND 3: *K6, K2 tog*, repeat around. (70 sts remain)

DECREASE RND 5: *K5, K2 tog*, repeat around. (60 sts remain)

DECREASE RND 7: *K4, K2 tog*, repeat around. (50 sts remain)

DECREASE RND 9: *K3, K2 tog*, repeat around. (40 sts remain)

DECREASE RND 11: *K2, K2 tog*, repeat around. (30 sts remain)

DECREASE RND 12: *K1, K2 tog*, repeat around. (20 sts remain)

DECREASE RND 13: *K2 tog*, repeat around. (10 sts remain)

I-CORD TASSELS: Place the remaining 10 sts on 3 safety pins as follows: 4 sts, 3 sts, 3 sts.

I-CORD TASSEL ROW 1: Place the 4 sts from the safety pin on a needle. Tie on purple. K2 tog, K across.

I-CORD TASSEL ROW 2: Slide the sts to the right side of the needle, bring the yarn from the back of the sts, tighten, and K across.

Repeat I-Cord Tassel Row 2 until tassel is 3 in. long. Tie off purple. Tie on orange. Work 4 rows of orange.

I-CORD TASSEL BIND-OFF: Sl 1, K2 tog, PSSO. Cut a 3-in. tail, thread the tail through the loop, and tighten. Weave the tails in on the inside of the tassel.

Repeat with the other tassels, omitting the decrease. Make one tassel tip blue and one tassel tip green.

FINISHING

With orange yarn in a large-eye needle, sew the top of the hat together at the base of the tassels. Weave the loose ends into the tassels. Weave the loose ends on the first ridge rnd into the ridge itself. Trim all other loose ends closely.

FELTING

Place the hat in a mesh zippered lingerie bag and wash on the hot/cold cycle. Check the progress frequently and remove the hat when the desired amount of felting has taken place. Hand-shape the hat so that the top is flat and the edges are straight and smooth. Smooth the I-cord tassels if necessary. Allow the hat to dry.

the Bobble Stitch

BOBBLE ROW 1:

Tie on bobble color, leaving a 3-in. tail. Pick up and knit 1, K1, pick up and knit 1. Turn. (3 bobble sts)

BOBBLE ROW 2:

Sl 1, P across. Turn.

BOBBLE ROW 3:

Sl 1, pick up and knit 1, K1, pick up and knit 1, K1. Turn. (5 bobble sts)

BOBBLE ROW 4:

Sl 1, P across. Turn.

BOBBLE ROW 5:

Sl 1, *K2 tog* twice. Turn.

BOBBLE ROW 6:

P3 tog. Turn.

Cut bobble yarn, leaving a 3-in. tail. Tie the 2 bobble tails together tightly, and trim closely. Leave the final bobble stitch on the left needle, and knit that st with the band color.

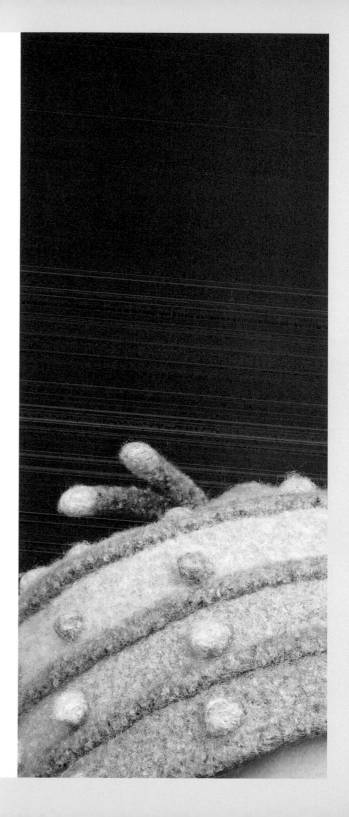

bobble scarf

You can use leftover yarn from the Bobble Bucket

Hat to knit this lightly felted matching scarf with raised ridges and bobble trim.

Yarn:
Cascade 220 Quatro, 100% Peruvian highland wool, 100 g, 220 yd., 1 skein each of #5011 (orange), #5019 (green), #5018 (blue), #5017 (purple)

Yarn Weight:
Worsted

Needles:
Size 11 (U.S.) straight, 14 in.

Tools:
Large-eye blunt needle

Size:
One size fits all

Unfelted Gauge:
3.5 sts = 1 in., 4 rnds = 1 in. in stockinette st

Number of Complete Washer Cycles to Felt us Shown:
(Adjust as necessary to achieve desired size.) Less than 1 Remove scarf from washer after 5 minutes of agitation.

Size before Felting:
47 in. long, 7 in. wide (scarf is knitted horizontally)

Size after Felting:
(NOTE: Sizes can vary due to individual washer cycles. Finished items that are too large can be felted again. Finished items that are too small can be stretched while wet to add about 15 percent additional length and/or width.) 50½ in. long, 4 in. wide

Number of Yarn Strands Used:
1 strand throughout

NOTE: Work bobbles as for Bobble Bucket Hat (see "The Bobble Stitch," on p. 35).

> **LONG, NARROW knitted pieces often gain length during the felting process.**

KNITTING INSTRUCTIONS

With purple and size 11 needles, CO 150 sts.

RIDGE ROWS 1 & 3: K.

RIDGE ROWS 2 & 4: P.

RIDGE ROW 5: With the tip of the left needle, reach to the back of the work and pick up one CO loop directly below the stitch. Knit those 2 loops together. Repeat across. Cut purple. Tie on orange.

BAND ROWS 1, 3, 5, 7: P.

BAND ROWS 2, 6: K.

BOBBLE ROW 4: Use blue for the bobbles. Work bobble on first st, K9 with orange, work bobble, K with orange to within 11 sts of the end, work bobble, K9 with orange, work bobble on last st.

Cut orange. Tie on purple.

Repeat purple ridge and band sections as for the Bobble Bucket Hat, working a blue band with green bobbles, a green band with orange bobbles, and a purple ridge between each band.

Work Ridge Rows 1–5.

RIDGE BIND-OFF ROW: With the tip of the left needle, reach to the back of the work and pick up the lowest purple loop directly below the first stitch. Knit those 2 loops together. With the tip of the left needle, reach to the back of the work and pick up the lowest purple loop directly below the next stitch. Knit those 2 loops together. Pass the first st over the 2nd st. Repeat across to BO.

FINISHING

Weave the loose ends on the ridge rows into the ridges themselves. Trim all other loose ends closely.

FELTING

Place the scarf in a mesh zippered lingerie bag and wash on the hot/cold cycle. Check the progress frequently and remove the scarf after about 5 minutes of agitation, or when the desired amount of felting has taken place. Rinse the scarf in warm water and spin or squeeze the excess moisture out. Note that long, narrow knitted pieces often gain length during the felting process. Smooth the scarf out flat so that the ridges and edges are straight, and the end bobbles protrude evenly. Allow the scarf to dry.

yellow ladders purse

Knit this lovely little bag in a flash, using a winning

combination of worsted-weight wool and ladder yarn. After felting, the ladder yarn really pops and adds a wonderful texture to the bag. Finish with purchased handles and a funky button.

Yarn:
Knit Picks® Wool of the Andes™, 100% Peruvian wool, 50 g, 110 yd., #23436 Daffodil, 2 skeins

Knit Picks Sparkles™, 100% nylon, 50 g, 159 yd., #23583 Sunset, 2 balls

Yarn Weight:
Worsted

Needles:
Size 13 (U.S.) dpn, 10 in.

Tools:
Large-eye blunt needle
Large-eye sharp needle
1 large stitch marker
Small stitch holder

Notions:
Matching thread
1¾ in. Clover Magnet Tote Bag Closure
One 1-in. button
1 set purchased purse handles

Unfelted Gauge:
3 sts = 1 in., 4 rows = 1 in. in stockinette st

Number of Complete Washer Cycles to Felt as Shown:
(Adjust as necessary to achieve desired size.) 1

Size before Felting:
Purse: 14½ in. wide at the bottom (lying flat), 11½ in. wide at the top (lying flat); flap: 6³⁄4 in. long, 3½ in. wide

Size after Felting:
(NOTE: Sizes can vary due to individual washer cycles. Finished items that are too large can be felted again. Finished items that are too small can be stretched while wet to add about 15 percent additional length and/or width.)
Purse: 10 in. wide at the widest point, 8 in. wide at the top, 6 in. tall (when sitting flat on the bottom); flap: 4 in. long, 2 in. wide

Number of Yarn Strands Used:
1 strand Wool of the Andes and 1 strand Sparkles held together throughout

KNITTING INSTRUCTIONS

With 1 strand Wool of the Andes and 1 strand Sparkles, CO 90 sts. Divide equally on 3 needles. Make sure that the stitches aren't twisted, and join.

RND 1: K. Work even until piece measures 10 in.

NEXT RND: K46, place marker, finish rnd.

SHAPING RND 1: K2 tog, K to within 2 sts of marker, K2 tog, slide marker, K2 tog, K to within 2 sts of end of rnd, K2 tog.

SHAPING RND 2: K. Repeat Shaping Rnds 1–2, 4 times. (70 sts rem)

Work even until piece measures 14 in.

NEXT RND: BO 12, K11 and then place those sts on a small stitch holder for the flap, BO all remaining sts.

Flap

Place the 11 sts on a needle. Work in stockinette stitch (K 1 row, P 1 row), until flap measures 6 in. End with a WS row.

NEXT ROW: BO 2, K Across.

NEXT ROW: BO 2, P Across.

Repeat these rows once.

BO remaining sts.

Shaping the Bottom

1. Lay the purse flat with the flap centered at the upper edge. Using a large-eye blunt needle and Wool of the Andes, sew the bottom seam together.

2. Turn the purse inside out, and flatten the corner as per the illustration at right. Measure 3 in. down either side of the corner, and sew a seam across the purse bottom at that point. Do not cut the excess fabric.

FELTING

Place the purse in a small mesh zippered lingerie bag and wash on the hot/cold cycle. Check the progress frequently and remove the purse when the desired amount of felting has taken place. The purse may need 1 or more complete washer cycles to reach the desired size. Remove the purse from the lingerie bag and pull it into shape, making the upper and flap edges straight and the flap point even. Trim any felted yarn ends flush with the fabric. Cut the excess fabric from the inside of the corners, and then hand-shape the purse and set it upright. Stuff lightly with plastic bags, if desired, to hold the shape. Allow to dry.

FINISHING

Following the instructions given on the magnetic closure package, apply the closure pieces to the center front of the bag and flap. You may need to fold the magnet flaps inward, rather than outward, so that the flaps are hidden completely by the button. Sew a decorative button over the closure on the flap. Using yarn and a large-eye sharp needle, sew the handles in place.

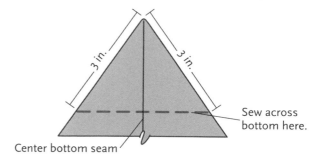

YELLOW LADDERS PURSE CORNER STITCHING DIAGRAM

child-size shaggy slippers

If fear of turning heels has kept you from making *felted slippers, then this is the perfect pattern for you. These adorable shaggy slippers have a flat bottom and no heel at all. Worked with strands of wool and novelty yarn, these slippers knit up in a flash. You can apply a nonskid bottom to these slippers, if you like.*

Yarn:
Brown Sheep Lamb's Pride Bulky, 85% wool/15% mohair, 4 oz. (113 g), 125 yd., #M120 Limeade, 1 skein
Crystal Palace Yarns Squiggle, 50% nylon/50% polyester, 50 g, 100 yd., #9547 Tulips, 1 skein

Yarn Weight:
Lamb's Pride Bulky: bulky; Squiggle: carry-along eyelash

Needles:
Size 11 (U.S.) dpn, 10 in.

Tools:
Large-eye blunt needle
Sewing needle

Notions:
Matching sewing thread

Sizes:
Youth size S, shoe size 12–13 (M, shoe size 1–2; L, shoe size 3–4); Average width (Wide)

Unfelted Gauge:
3 sts = 1 in., 4 rows = 1 in. in stockinette st

Number of Complete Washer Cycles to Felt as Shown:
(Adjust as necessary to achieve desired size.) 2 for slippers, 1 for I-cord

Sizes before Felting:
5 in. (5½ in.) wide, lying flat; 14 in. (15 in., 16 in.) long

Sizes after Felting:
(NOTE: Sizes can vary due to individual washer cycles. Finished items that are too large can be felted again. Finished items that are too small can be stretched while wet to add about 15 percent additional length and/or width.)
Approx 7 in. (8 in., 9 in.) long

Number of Yarn Strands Used:
1 strand Lamb's Pride Bulky and 1 strand Squiggle for slippers, 1 strand Lamb's Pride Bulky for I-cord

KNITTING INSTRUCTIONS

Slipper (make 2)

With 1 strand of Lamb's Pride Bulky and 1 strand of Squiggle held together, CO 15.

ROW 1: K across, turn.

ROW 2: CO 1, P across, turn. (16 sts)

ROW 3: CO 1, K across, turn. (17 sts)

Rep Rows 2–3 until there are 24 (26) sts on the needle. Work even in stockinette st for 5 rows. End with a purl row.

NEXT ROW: CO 6 sts, divide all sts as evenly as possible on 3 needles, join. (30, 32 sts)

FOOT RND 1: K.

Work even until slipper measures 9½ in. (10½ in., 11½ in.).

LAST RND (WIDE ONLY): Dec 2 sts. (30 sts)

TOE DECREASE RND 1: *K8, K2 tog*, repeat around.

TOE DECREASE RND 2 AND ALL EVEN DECREASE RNDS: K.

TOE DECREASE RND 3: *K7, K2 tog*, repeat around.

TOE DECREASE RND 5: *K6, K2 tog*, repeat around.

Continue decreasing every other rnd in this manner until 12 sts remain.

NEXT RND: *K2 tog*, repeat around.

Cut a 12-in. tail of yarn. Thread the tail in a large-eye needle, weave through the remaining sts, and tie off. Weave the end in on the knit side of the slipper. Weave all loose ends in on the knit side of the slipper.

Turn the slipper so that the purl side is out. Pull the Squiggle eyelashes to the purl side of the slipper by hand-brushing the surface to loosen the eyelash ends. This is a little tedious, but it goes pretty quickly, and it makes a difference in what the slipper looks like.

I-Cord (make 2)

With Lamb's Pride Bulky and size 11 needles, CO 3 sts.

ROW 1: K across. Do not turn.

ROW 2: Slide the sts to the right side of the needle. Bring the yarn around from the back, and K across. Rep Row 2 until the I-cord is 36 in. long.

LAST ROW: Sl 1, K2 tog, PSSO. Cut a 4-in. tail of yarn. Thread the tail in a large-eye needle and weave the tail through the final loop and tighten. Tie off and weave the tails inside the I-cord.

FELTING

Turn the slippers purl side out, place them and the I-cords in a mesh zippered lingerie bag, and wash on the hot/cold cycle. Check the progress frequently and remove the slippers and I-cord when the desired amount of felting has taken place. Remove the slippers from the lingerie bag and pull them into shape, flattening the bottom and rounding the foot. Stuff with plastic bags to hold shape, if desired. Allow to dry.

NOTE ABOUT FIT: These slippers can be easily adjusted for individual sizes. If they seem too short or tight, pull on the bottom and/or sides to stretch them while they're still wet. If they're too loose and long, felt another cycle.

If they're the right width but too long, the excess length can be trimmed from the heel portion after the slippers are shaped and dried. Do not trim the back too short; allow for socks to be worn with the slippers.

ASSEMBLY

After the slippers and I-cords have dried, adjust the slipper length by trimming the heel section, if necessary. Trim the sides and foot opening, if necessary, to make the slope even.

With matching sewing thread, beginning at the center back of the heel, sew the I-cord to the foot opening. Stitch around the inside and the outside of the I-cord to anchor it fully. Trim the I-cord to fit. Tie a knot in the center of the remaining I-cord and tack it to the center top of the slipper opening. Trim the I-cord ends if necessary.

OPTIONAL: Trim the eyelashes flush with the outside bottom of the slipper and sew purchased slipper bottoms on. You can also paint the trimmed slipper bottom with a nonskid medium such as Plasti Dip® or Puff Paint. Follow the directions given with the nonskid medium.

THE PURL SIDE (inside when working in the round) is the right side. Most of the eyelash portions will automatically end up on the purl side of the work.

"it looks like a purse"

When I was designing prototypes for the Shaggy Slippers

I had a misfire or two as I worked out the kinks in the pattern. One of the misfires looked particularly silly as a slipper, but my husband squinted at it and said, "It looks like a purse to me." He was right. It did look like a purse, and a darned cute one at that. I used the same yarn as the Child-Size Shaggy Slippers, but you can use any fellable worsted-weight wool yarn and any eyelash yarn, about 100 yards of each, to make your own little bag. Be sure to use a funky button to dress up the finished bag.

Yarn:
Brown Sheep Lamb's Pride Bulky, 85% wool/15% mohair, 4 oz. (113 g), 125 yd., #M120 Limeade, approx. 100 yd.
Crystal Palace Yarns Squiggle, 50% nylon/50% polyester, 50 g, 100 yd., #9547 Tulips, 1 skein

Yarn Weight:
Lamb's Pride Bulky: bulky; Squiggle: carry-along eyelash

Needles:
Size 11 (U.S.) dpn, 10 in.

Tools:
Large-eye blunt needle
Sewing needle

Notions:
Matching sewing thread
1-in. button

Unfelted Gauge:
3 sts = 1 in., 4 rows = 1 in. in stockinette st. (NOTE: Gauge is not particularly important on this project.)

Number of Complete Washer Cycles to Felt as Shown:
(Adjust as necessary to achieve desired size.) 2 for bag, 1 for I-cord

Size before Felting:
14 in. long. (NOTE: Length is not particularly important on this project.)

Size after Felting:
(NOTE: Size can vary due to individual washer cycles. Finished items that are too large can be felted again. Finished items that are too small can be stretched while wet, to add about 15 percent additional length and/or width.)
Approx. 7 in. wide, approx. 8½ in. long (including flap)

Number of Yarn Strands Used:
1 strand Lamb's Pride Bulky and 1 strand Squiggle for purse, 1 strand Lamb's Pride Bulky for I-cord

KNITTING INSTRUCTIONS

With 1 strand of Lamb's Pride Bulky and 1 strand of Squiggle held together, CO 10.

FLAP ROW 1: K across, turn.

FLAP ROW 2: P across, turn.

Rep Flap Rows 1–2, 3 times.

BAG ROW 1: CO 2, K across, turn. (12 sts)

BAG ROW 2: CO 2, P across, turn. (14 sts)

Rep Bag Rows 1–2 until there are 30 sts. End with a purl row. Turn.

NEXT ROW: CO 18 sts, divide all sts evenly on 3 needles, join. (48 sts)

BAG RND 1: K.

Work even until bag portion measures 10 in.

DECREASE RND 1: *K6, K2 tog*, repeat around.

DECREASE RND 2 AND ALL EVEN DECREASE RNDS: K.

DECREASE RND 3: *K5, K2 tog*, repeat around.

DECREASE RND 5: *K4, K2 tog*, repeat around.

Continue decreasing every other rnd in this manner until 12 sts rem.

NEXT RND: *K2 tog*, repeat around.

Cut a 12-in. tail of yarn. Thread the tail in a large-eye needle, weave through the remaining sts, and tie off. Weave the end in on the knit side of the bag. Weave all loose ends in on the knit side of the bag.

Turn the bag so that the purl side is out. Pull the Squiggle eyelashes to the purl side of the bag.

I-Cord (make 1):

With Lamb's Pride Bulky and size 11 needles, CO 3 sts.

ROW 1: K across. Do not turn.

ROW 2: Slide the sts to the right side of the needle. Bring the yarn around from the back, and K across.

Rep Row 2 until the I-cord is 36 in. long.

LAST ROW: Sl 1, K2 tog, PSSO. Cut a 4-in. tail of yarn. Thread the tail in a large-eye needle and weave the tail through the final loop and tighten. Tie off and weave the tails inside the I-cord.

FELTING

Place the I-cord and bag with purl side out in a mesh zippered lingerie bag and wash on the hot/cold cycle. Check the progress frequently and remove the pieces when the desired amount of felting has taken place. Remove pieces from the lingerie bag and pull them into shape. Stuff the bag with plastic bags to hold shape if desired. Allow to dry.

ASSEMBLY

After the felted bag and I-cord have dried, sew the I-cord to either side of the bag as a handle. Cut a 1-in. slit, centered, 1 in. in from the edge of the flap. Sew a 1-in. button on the center front upper edge of the bag.

alpaca for him: adult hat

The muted, heathered tones of this lovely

100 percent alpaca yarn blend perfectly in this amazingly soft man's hat.

Yarn:
Knit Picks Andean Treasure™, 100% baby alpaca, 50 g, 110 yd., #23494 Mystery, 2 balls; #23490 Fog, #23486 Embers, #23488 Granite, #23491 Woods, 1 ball each
Note: If you are knitting a complete Alpaca for Him Adult and Toddler set, 1 ball each of Fog, Embers, Granite, and Woods will be sufficient for the stripes on both hats and the scarf.

Yarn Weight:
DK

Needles:
Size 9 (U.S.) dpn, 10 in.

Tools:
Large-eye blunt needle

Size:
Adult

Unfelted Gauge:
Approx 5 sts = 1 in., 6 rnds = 1 in. in stockinette st

Number of Complete Washer Cycles to Felt as Shown:
(Adjust as necessary to achieve desired size.) Less than 1. Remove hat after about 7 minutes of agitation. Rinse in warm water.

Size before Felting:
13 in. wide (lying flat), 13 in. from lower edge to top

Size after Felting:
(NOTE: Sizes can vary due to individual washer cycles. Finished items that are too large can be felted again. Finished items that are too small can be stretched while wet to add about 15 percent additional length and/or width.) 12 in. wide (lying flat), 9 in. from lower edge to top

Number of Yarn Strands Used:
1 throughout
NOTE: Do not strand yarn up the side of the work at color changes. Cut and tie the yarn at each color change.

Stripe Pattern Repeat:
8 rnds Mystery, 2 rnds Granite, 2 rnds Embers, 2 rnds Granite, 8 rnds Mystery, 2 rnds Fog, 2 rnds Woods, 2 rnds Fog

KNITTING INSTRUCTIONS

With Mystery and size 9 needles, CO 110 sts. Divide as evenly as possible on 3 dpn. Making sure the sts are not twisted, join.

Rnd 1: K.

Work even for 9 in., working one entire Stripe Pattern Repeat, then another Granite/Embers band, then continue with Mystery.

DECREASE RND 1: *K9, K2 tog*, repeat around. (100 sts remain)

DECREASE RND 2 AND ALL EVEN DECREASE RNDS UNTIL OTHERWISE NOTED: K.

DECREASE RND 3: *K8, K2 tog*, repeat around. (90 sts remain)

DECREASE RND 5: *K7, K2 tog*, repeat around. (80 sts remain)

DECREASE RND 7: *K6, K2 tog*, repeat around. (70 sts remain)

DECREASE RND 9: *K5, K2 tog*, repeat around. (60 sts remain)

DECREASE RND 11: *K4, K2 tog*, repeat around. (50 sts remain)

DECREASE RND 13: *K3, K2 tog*, repeat around. (40 sts remain)

DECREASE RND 15: *K2, K2 tog*, repeat around. (30 sts remain)

DECREASE RND 17: *K1, K2 tog*, repeat around. (20 sts remain)

DECREASE RND 18: *K2 tog*, repeat around. (10 sts remain)

Cut the yarn leaving a 12-in. tail. Thread the tail in a large-eye needle, weave through the remaining stitches, and tighten. Tie off on the inside of the hat.

ALPACA is a very slippery fiber, and knots can come undone during the felting process, leaving holes that need to be stitched together later. Tighten all of the knots at the color changes, but do not cut the tails until after felting.

FELTING

Place hat in a mesh zippered lingerie bag and wash on the hot/cold cycle. Remove the hat when the desired amount of felting has taken place. Rinse in warm water and spin excess moisture out. Remove from lingerie bag and pull the hat into shape, using a head form if desired. Pull the edges straight. Trim all of the felted knots and yarn tail ends. Allow the hat to dry.

NOTE: This yarn sheds quite a bit during the felting process. Do not felt alpaca items with items made of any other yarn. Check the hat frequently; once the shrinking process begins, alpaca yarn felts almost instantly.

alpaca for him: scarf

Knit and lightly felt a wonderfully soft scarf

to coordinate with the felted alpaca hats.

Yarn:
Knit Picks® Andean Treasure, 100% baby alpaca, 50 g, 110 yd., #23494 Mystery, 2 balls; #23490 Fog, #23480 Embers, #23488 Granite, #23491 Woods, 1 ball each
NOTE: If you are knitting a complete Alpaca for Him Adult and Toddler set, 1 ball each of Fog, Embers, Granite, and Woods will be sufficient for the stripes on both hats and the scarf.

Yarn Weight:
DK

Needles:
Size 9 (U.S.) straight, 10 in.

Size:
One size fits all

Unfelted Gauge:
Approx 5 sts = 1 in., 6 rnds = 1 in. in stockinette st

Number of Complete Washer Cycles to Felt as Shown:
(Adjust as necessary to achieve the desired size.) Less than 1. Remove the scarf after 5 minutes of agitation. Rinse in warm water.

Size before Felting:
Approx 6 in. wide, 53½ in. long

Size after Felting:
(NOTE: Sizes can vary due to individual washer cycles. Finished items that are too large can be felted again. Finished items that are too small can be stretched while wet to add about 15 percent additional length and/or width.) 4¾ in. wide, 44½ in. long.

Number of Yarn Strands Used:
1 throughout
NOTE: Do not strand yarn up the side of the work at color changes. Cut and tie the yarn at each color change.

Stripe Pattern Repeat:
20 rows Mystery, 4 rows Granite, 4 rows Embers, 4 rows Granite, 20 rows Mystery, 4 rows Fog, 4 rows Woods, 4 rows Fog

KNITTING INSTRUCTIONS

With Mystery and size 9 needles, CO 28 sts.
Work in stockinette st throughout, following the Stripe Pattern Repeat twice. End with 20 rows of Mystery (or continue for desired length).

BO all sts. Do not weave ends in.

Alpaca is a very slippery fiber, and knots can come undone during the felting process, leaving holes that need to be stitched together later. Tighten all of the knots at the color changes, but do not cut them or weave the ends in.

AS A RULE, LONG, NARROW KNITTED PIECES GAIN LENGTH during the felting process, but that is not the case with this scarf because alpaca yarn felts very easily and quickly.

FELTING

This item should only be lightly felted. Place scarf in a mesh zippered lingerie bag and wash on the hot/cold cycle. Check the scarf frequently. Remove the scarf when the desired amount of felting has taken place. Rinse in warm water and spin excess moisture out. Flatten the scarf, pulling it into shape. Make sure the edges and stripes are straight. Trim all of the felted knots and yarn tail ends. Allow the scarf to dry.

NOTE: This yarn sheds quite a bit during the felting process. Do not felt alpaca items with items made from any other yarn.

alpaca for him:
toddler earflap hat

Make a father-and-son set by knitting
this next-to-skin-soft earflap hat for the little one in his life.

Yarn:
Knit Picks Andean Treasure, 100% baby alpaca, 50 g, 110 yd., #23494 Mystery, 2 balls; #23490 Fog, #23486 Embers, #23488 Granite, #23491 Woods, 1 ball each
NOTE: If you are knitting a complete Alpaca for Him Adult and Toddler set, 1 ball each of Fog, Embers, Granite, and Woods will be sufficient for the stripes on both hats and the scarf.

Yarn Weight:
DK

Needles:
Size 9 (U.S.) dpn, 10 in.

Tools:
Large-eye blunt needle

Size: Toddler

Unfelted Gauge:
Approx 5 sts = 1 in., 6 rnds = 1 in. in stockinette st

Number of Complete Washer Cycles to Felt as Shown:
(Adjust as necessary to achieve the desired size.) Less than 1. Remove hat after about 7 minutes of agitation. Rinse in warm water.

Size before Felting:
11 in. wide (lying flat), 8¼ in. from brim edge to top, 14 in. from earflap lower edge to top, 10½-in. I-cord

Size after Felting:
(NOTE: Sizes can vary due to individual washer cycles. Finished items that are too large can be felted again. Finished items that are too small can be stretched while wet to add about 15 percent additional length and/or width.) 9 in. wide (lying flat), 6½ in. from front edge to top, 8¾ in. from earflap lower edge to top, 8-in. I-cord

Number of Yarn Strands Used:
1 throughout
NOTE: Do not strand yarn up the side of the work at color changes. Cut and tie the yarn at each color change.

Stripe Pattern Repeat:
8 rows/rnds Mystery, 2 rows/rnds Granite, 2 rows/rnds Embers, 2 rows/rnds Granite, 8 rows/rnds Mystery, 2 rows/rnds Fog, 2 rows/rnds Woods, 2 rows/rnds Fog

KNITTING INSTRUCTIONS

Earflap (make 2)

With Mystery and size 9 dpn, cast on 3 sts.

I-CORD ROW 1: K across.

I-CORD ROW 2: Slide the sts to the right side of the needle, bring the yarn from the back of the sts, and tighten. K across.

Repeat Row 2 until the I-cord is 10½ in. long.

EARFLAP ROW 1: Turn. P across. Turn.

EARFLAP ROW 2: K1, inc 1, K1, inc 1, K1. Turn. (2 sts increased)

EARFLAP ROW 3 AND ALL ODD ROWS UNTIL OTHERWISE NOTED: P across. Turn.

EARFLAP ROW 4: K1, inc 1, K to within 1 of the end, inc 1, K1. Turn. (2 sts increased)

Repeat Earflap Rows 3–4 until there are 33 sts on the needle. As you knit, work one entire Stripe Pattern Repeat, and then continue with Mystery. End with a purl row. Cut yarn, leaving a 10-in. tail.

Hat

With Mystery, CO 18 sts, K 33 sts from 1 earflap, CO 16 sts, K 33 sts from other earflap. Divide as evenly as possible on 3 or 4 dpn, as desired. (100 sts)

RND 1: K.

Work even for 6 in., working one entire Stripe Pattern Repeat, then continue with Mystery.

DECREASE RND 1: *K8, K2 tog*, repeat around. (90 sts remain)

DECREASE RND 2 AND ALL EVEN DECREASE RNDS UNTIL OTHERWISE NOTED: K.

DECREASE RND 3: *K7, K2 tog*, repeat around. (80 sts remain)

DECREASE RND 5: *K6, K2 tog*, repeat around. (70 sts remain)

DECREASE RND 7: *K5, K2 tog*, repeat around. (60 sts remain)

DECREASE RND 9: *K4, K2 tog*, repeat around. (50 sts remain)

DECREASE RND 11: *K3, K2 tog*, repeat around. (40 sts remain)

DECREASE RND 13: *K2, K2 tog*, repeat around. (30 sts remain)

DECREASE RND 15: *K1, K2 tog*, repeat around. (20 sts remain)

DECREASE RND 16: *K2 tog*, repeat around. (10 sts remain)

Cut the yarn, leaving a 12-in. tail. Thread the tail in a large-eye needle, weave through the remaining stitches, and tighten. Tie off on the inside of the hat.

Weave in the ends on the I-cords.

Alpaca is a very slippery fiber and knots can come undone during the felting process, leaving holes that need to be stitched together later. Tighten all of the knots at the color changes, but do not cut them or weave the ends in.

FELTING

Place hat in a mesh zippered lingerie bag and wash on the hot/cold cycle. Remove the hat when desired amount of felting has taken place. Rinse in warm water and spin excess moisture out. Remove the hat from the lingerie bag and pull it into shape, using a small mannequin head if desired. Pull the upper edges, earflaps, and I-cords straight. Trim all of the felted knots and yarn tail ends. Allow the hat to dry.

NOTE: This yarn sheds quite a bit during the felting process. Do not felt alpaca items with items made of any other yarn. Check the hat frequently; once the shrinking process begins, alpaca yarn felts almost instantly.

alpaca for her:
cranberry honeycomb scarf

Enjoy the luxury of this wonderful
alpaca-blend yarn in this lightly felted honeycomb-cable scarf.

Yarn:
Knit Picks Cadena, 70% wool/ 30% superfine alpaca, 100 g, 110 yd., #23783 Cranberry, 2 skeins

Yarn Weight:
Bulky

Needles:
Size 15 (U.S.) straight, 10 in.
Large cable needle

Tools:
Large-eye blunt needle

Size:
One size fits all

Unfelted Gauge:
26 sts = 6 in., 4 rows = 1 in. in cable pattern

Number of Complete Washer Cycles to Felt as Shown:
(Adjust as necessary to achieve the desired size.) Less than 1. Remove scarf after about 5 minutes of agitation.

Size before Felting:
6 in. wide, 43 in. long

Size after Felting:
(NOTE: Sizes can vary due to individual washer cycles. Finished items that are too large can be felted again. Finished items that are too small can be stretched while wet to add about 15 percent additional length and/or width.)
5 in. wide, 46 in. long

Number of Yarn Strands Used:
1 throughout
NOTE: It is the nature of long, narrow knitted items to gain length during the felting process.

Cable Stitch Instructions:
4RT = 4-st Right Twist:
Place the first 2 sts on a cable needle and hold behind the work. Knit the next 2 sts. Place the first 2 sts on the left needle, and knit them.
4LT = 4-st Left Twist:
Place the first 2 sts on a cable needle and hold in front of the work. Knit the next 2 sts. Place the first 2 sts on the left needle, and knit them.

KNITTING INSTRUCTIONS

With size 15 needles, CO 26 sts.

ROW 1: K.

ROW 2: P.

ROW 3: K1, *4RT, 4LT*, repeat across, end K1.

ROW 4: P.

ROW 5: K.

ROW 6: P.

ROW 7: K 1, *4LT, 4RT*, repeat across, end K1.

ROW 8: P.

Repeat these 8 rows until scarf measures 43 in.

BO. Weave loose ends in.

FELTING

Place scarf in a mesh zippered lingerie bag and wash on the hot/cold cycle. Check the progress frequently and remove the scarf after 5 minutes of agitation, or after desired amount of felting has taken place. Remove scarf from lingerie bag and gently shape it, making edges and cables straight. Allow scarf to dry.

WARNING: I observed a little dye run while felting this yarn. Do not felt with projects worked in different colors.

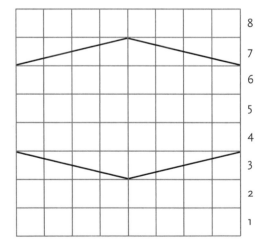

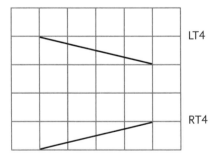

CRANBERRY HONEYCOMB SCARF CABLE CHART

alpaca for her:
cranberry honeycomb ear warmer

Knit a matching adjustable ear warmer

to go with the Cranberry Honeycomb Scarf. Wear it with the buttons showing, or hide the buttons under your hair.

Yarn:
Knit Picks Cadena, 70% wool/ 30% superfine alpaca, 100 g, 110 yd., #23783 Cranberry, 1 skein

Yarn Weight:
Bulky

Needles:
Size 15 (U.S.) straight, 10 in
Large cable needle

Tools:
Large-eye blunt needle
Sewing needle

Notions:
Two 1-in. buttons
Matching thread

Size:
One size fits all

Unfelted Gauge:
18 sts = 4¼ in., 4 rows = 1 in. in cable pattern

Number of Complete Washer Cycles to Felt as Shown:
(Adjust as necessary to achieve desired size.) Less than 1. Remove after 5 minutes of agitation.

Size before Felting:
4¼ in. wide, 24 in. long

Size after Felting:
(NOTE: Sizes can vary due to individual washer cycles. Finished items that are too large can be felted again. Finished items that are too small can be stretched while wet to add about 15 percent additional length and/or width.)
3¾ in. wide, 25 in. long

Number of Yarn Strands Used:
1 throughout

NOTE: It is the nature of long, narrow knitted items to gain length during the felting process. See Cranberry Honeycomb Scarf for cable stitch definitions (p. 59). Lightly felted items cannot be trimmed without raveling.

KNITTING INSTRUCTIONS

With size 15 needles, CO 18 sts.

ROW 1: K.

ROW 2: P.

ROW 3: K1, *4RT, 4LT*, repeat across, end K1.

ROW 4 BUTTONHOLES: P4, BO 2, P6, BO 2, P4.

ROW 5 BUTTONHOLES: K4, CO 2, K6, CO 2, K4.

ROW 6: P.

ROW 7: K 1, *4LT, 4RT*, repeat across, end K1.

ROW 8: P.

ROW 9: K.

ROW 10: P.

ROW 11: K1, *4RT, 4LT*, repeat across, end K1.

ROW 12: P.

ROW 13: K.

ROW 14: P.

ROW 15: K 1, *4LT, 4RT*, repeat across, end K1.

ROW 16: P.

Rep rows 9–16 until piece measures 24 in.

BO. Weave loose ends in.

FELTING

Place ear warmer in a mesh zippered lingerie bag and wash on the hot/cold cycle. Check the progress frequently and remove the ear warmer after 5 minutes of agitation, or after desired amount of felting has taken place. Remove the piece from the lingerie bag and gently shape it, making edges and cables straight. Allow to dry.

FINISHING

Fit ear warmer around head. Adjust overlap and sew two 1-in. buttons in place.

cabled tote

Knitted felt doesn't have to be made from plain

stockinette stitch. Cable designs show up perfectly on lightly felted fabric. A good example is this handy tote, knit in a beautiful spring green and lined with an inexpensive purchased canvas buy for strength and durability.

Yarn:

Knit Picks Cadena, 70% wool/30% superfine alpaca, 100 g, 110 yd., #23787 Leaf, 3 skeins

Yarn Weight:

Bulky

Needles:

Size 15 (U.S.) straight needles, 14 in.

Tools:

Large-eye blunt needle
Sewing needle

Notions:

Off-white sewing thread
Purchased canvas tote bag: 13½ in. by 13½ in.
1¾-in. Clover Magnet

Tote Bag Closure

Purchased bag handles

Unfelted Gauge on Stockinette Portions:

2.5 sts = 1 in., 3.5 rows = 1 in.

Number of Complete Washer Cycles to Felt as Shown:

(Adjust as necessary to achieve desired size.) Less than 1. Remove piece after about 5 minutes of agitation.

Felted Size after Assembly:

Approx. 14 in. tall, 13 in. wide, lying flat

Number of Yarn Strands Used:

1 throughout

Unfelted Size before Assembly:

UNFELTED

10½ in.

16 in.

3½ in.

16 in.

4 in.

35½ in. total length and 18½ in. total width before felting

FELTED

10 in.

Tote back

13 in.

Tote bottom

B

A

2¾ in.

Tote side

A

Tote front

B

13 in.

2¾ in.

Felted measurements taken after assembly, felting, and blocking.

CABLED TOTE MEASUREMENTS

CABLE STITCH INSTRUCTIONS

6RT = 6-ST RIGHT TWIST: Place 4 sts (K2, P2) on a cable needle, hold behind work, K2, transfer the 2 P sts from the cable needle to the left needle, P those sts, transfer the 2 K sts from the cable needle to the left needle, K those sts.

6LT = 6-ST LEFT TWIST: Place 4 sts (K2, P2) on a cable needle, hold in front of work, K2, transfer the 2 P sts from the cable needle to the left needle, P those sts, transfer the 2 K sts from the cable needle to the left needle, K those sts.

4LT = 4-ST LEFT TWIST: Place 2 K sts on a cable needle, hold in front of work, K2, transfer the 2 K sts from the cable needle to the left needle, K those sts.

3RT = 3-ST RIGHT TWIST: Place 1 P st on a cable needle, hold behind work, K2, transfer the 1 P st from the cable needle to the left needle, P that st.

3LT = 3-ST LEFT TWIST: Place 2 K sts on a cable needle, hold in front of work, P1, transfer the 2 K sts to the left needle, K those sts.

BOBBLE INSTRUCTIONS

ROW 1: K1, inc 1, K1, inc 1, turn.
ROW 2: P4, turn.
ROW 3: *K1, inc 1*, 4 times, turn.
ROW 4: P8, turn.
ROW 5: *K2 tog* 4 times, turn.
ROW 6: *P2 tog* 2 times, turn.
ROW 7: P2, continue with row.

20-ROW PATTERN REPEAT

NOTE: On WS, K the K sts, P the P sts throughout.
ROW 1 (RS): P4, 6RT, P8, 4LT, P8, 6LT, P4.
ROW 2 (WS): K4, P2, K2, P2, K8, P4, K8, P2, K2, P2, K4.
ROW 3: P4, K2, P2, K2, P7, 3RT, 3LT, P7, K2, P2, K2, P4.
ROW 4: K4, P2, K2, P2, K7, P2, K2, P2, K7, P2, K2, P2, K4.
ROW 5: P4, K2, P2, K2, P6, 3RT, P2, 3LT, P6, K2, P2, K2, P4.
ROW 6: K4, P2, K2, P2, K6, P2, K4, P2, K6, P2, K2, P2, K4.
ROW 7: P4, K2, P2, K2, P5, 3RT, P4, 3LT, P5, K2, P2, K2, P4.
ROW 8: K4, P2, K2, P2, K5, P2, K6, P2, K5, P2, K2, P2, K4.
ROW 9: P4, K2, P2, K2, P4, 3RT, P6, 3LT, P4, K2, P2, K2, P4.
ROW 10: K4, P2, K2, P2, K4, P2, K8, P2, K4, P2, K2, P2, K4.
ROW 11: P4, 6RT, P4, K2, P3, make bobble, P3, K2, P4, 6LT, P4.
ROW 12: K4, P2, K2, P2, K4, P2, K8, P2, K4, P2, K2, P2, K4.
ROW 13: P4, K2, P2, K2, P4, 3LT, P6, 3RT, P4, K2, P2, K2, P4.
ROW 14: K4, P2, K2, P2, K5, P2, K6, P2, K5, P2, K2, P2, K4.
ROW 15: P4, K2, P2, K2, P5, 3LT, P4, 3RT, P5, K2, P2, K2, P4.
ROW 16: K4, P2, K2, P2, K6, P2, K4, P2, K6, P2, K2, P2, K4.
ROW 17: P4, K2, P2, K2, P6, 3RT, P2, 3LT, P6, K2, P2, K2, P4.
ROW 18: K4, P2, K2, P2, K7, P2, K2, P2, K7, P2, K2, P2, K4.
ROW 19: P4, K2, P2, K2, P7, 3LT, 3RT, P7, K2, P2, K2, P4.
ROW 20: K4, P2, K2, P2, K8, P4, K8, P2, K2, P2, K4.

KNITTING INSTRUCTIONS

NOTE: The bag body is knit in one piece, as follows:
With size 15 needles, CO 40 sts.

Tote Back
SET-UP ROW (WS): K4, P2, K2, P2, K8, P4, K8, P2, K2, P2, K4.

Follow chart for 3 full repeats, or follow the text instructions for 3 full repeats for Tote Back.

Tote Bottom

Work even (no cables or bobbles) for 12 rows, ending with a RS row. CO 10 sts at end of row.

Tote Sides and Front

NEXT ROW (RS): P the CO sts, work even across original 40 sts, CO 10 sts at end of row.

Work 3 more repeats of the chart, working all of the Tote Side sts as follows: P on RS, K on WS.

BO in pattern.

ASSEMBLY

Using yarn in a large-eye blunt needle, stitch the Tote Bottoms A to Tote Sides A as shown in the illustration at left on p. 65. You may need to ease the Tote Bottom a bit to fit the Tote Side A. Using yarn in a large-eye blunt needle, stitch Tote Sides B together as shown in the illustration at right on p. 65. Push the bobbles out so that they extend on the right side of the work.

FELTING

Place bag in a mesh zippered lingerie bag and wash on the hot/cold cycle. Check the progress frequently and remove the bag after 5 minutes of agitation, or after desired amount of felting has taken place. Remove bag from lingerie bag and gently shape it, making edges and cables straight. Allow bag to dry.

FINISHING

Trim the handles from the purchased canvas tote bag and discard them. Apply the ¾-in. magnetic closure to the center top of the canvas bag as per the manufacturer's instructions. Fit the canvas tote bag, RS in, inside the felted tote and whipstitch the upper edge of the canvas tote ¼ in. down from the inside upper edge of the felted tote. Using yarn in a large-eye needle, sew on the bag handles so that they are centered over the small cables.

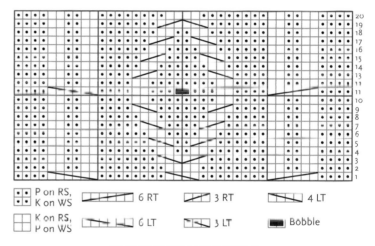

CABLED TOTE CABLE CHART

P on RS, K on WS	6 RT	3 RT	4 LT	
K on RS, P on WS	6 LT	3 LT	Bobble	

cabled evergreen jacket

Ward off chills with this lovely cabled jacket,

which has a lightly felted body and contrasting unfelted sleeves. The body of the jacket is worked in a single piece, with the sleeve openings and neck shaping cut after felting.

Yarn:
Knit Picks Wool of the Andes Bulky Hand Dyed™, 100% Peruvian wool, 100 g, 137 yd., #23952 Ireland, 6 (6, 7, 8) skeins
Knit Picks Wool of the Andes Bulky™, 100% Peruvian wool, 100 g, 137 yd., #23957 Emerald 4 (4, 5, 5) skeins

Yarn Weight:
Bulky

Needles:
Size 10 (U.S.) straight, 10 in.
Size 11 (U.S.) straight, 14 in., or 24-in. circular. Size 13 (U.S.) circular needle, 32 in. (or longer)
Cable needle

Tools:
Large-eye blunt needle
Large-eye sharp needle
Sewing needle

Notions:
Eight 1-in. buttons
Matching thread
NOTE: A sewing machine is handy for reinforcing the steeks at the armholes and neckline since lightly felted fabric may ravel. However, you can reinforce the cut edges with whip-stitching by hand, if desired.

Sizes:
Ladies S (M, L, XL)

Unfelted Gauge:
3 sts = 1 in., 3.5 rows = 1 in. in stockinette st with size 13 needles

Sleeve Gauge:
3.25 sts=1 in., 4.5 rows=1 in. in sleeve pattern with size 11 needles

Number of Complete Washer Cycles to Felt as Shown:
(Adjust as necessary to achieve desired size.) Less than 1. Remove after 8 minutes of agitation.

Sizes before Felting:

30 in. long (all sizes), 36 in. (40 in., 44 in., 48 in.) wide, lying flat.

Sizes after Felting:

(NOTE: Sizes can vary due to individual washer cycles. Finished items that are too large can be felted again. Finished items that are too small can be stretched while wet, to add about 15 percent additional length and/or width.) 27 in. long (before bottom band is added) all sizes; 40 in. (44 in., 48 in., 52 in.) wide lying flat; armhole depth: 10½ in. (10½ in., 11½ in., 11½ in.)

Unfelted Sleeve Sizes:

22 in. long for all sizes; ribbing 2¾ in. long for all sizes; 20 in. (20 in., 22 in., 22 in.) wide at widest point

Number of Yarn Strands Used:

1 throughout

NOTE ABOUT WIDTH BEFORE FELTING: Width is measured without stretching the knitted fabric.

NOTE ABOUT WIDTH AFTER FELTING: Light felting will relax the ribbing and cables so the felted fabric will be wider than before felting. You must block the body rectangle to the proper measurements while wet.

CABLE STITCH INSTRUCTIONS

6LT = 6-st Left Twist: Place the first 4 cable sts (K2, P2) on the cable needle, hold the cable needle in front of the work, K the next 2 sts, place the 2 P sts from the cable needle on the left needle and P them, place the 2 K sts from the cable needle sts on the left needle and K them.

KNITTING INSTRUCTIONS

With size 13 circular needle and Ireland, CO 118 (134, 150, 166) sts. Work the following back and forth (do not join).

SET-UP ROW 1 (WS): K7 (8, 9, 10), *P2, K2, P2, K3 (4, 5, 6), P2, K3 (4, 5, 6)* 7 times, P2, K2, P2, K7 (8, 9, 10).

ROW 2 (RS): P7 (8, 9, 10), *K2, P2, K2, P3 (4, 5, 6), K2, P3 (4, 5, 6)* 7 times, K2, P2, K2, P7 (8, 9, 10).

ROW 3: Rep Row 1.

ROW 4 (CABLE ROW): K7 (8, 9, 10), *6LT, P3 (4, 5, 6), K2, P3 (4, 5, 6)* 7 times, 6LT, P7 (8, 9, 10). Continue in pattern, working a Cable Row every 6th row on the right side, until piece measures 30 in. BO in pattern.

Sleeves (make 2)

NOTE: Size S/M are worked the same. Sizes L/XL are worked the same.

With size 10 needles and Emerald, CO 32 (38) sts. Work K1, P1 ribbing for 15 rows.

ROW 16 (WS, ALL SIZES): Inc 10 sts evenly across the row. (42, 48 sts)

ROW 17 (RS, S/M ONLY): Change to size 11 needles. *K2, P8* twice, K2, *P8, K2* twice.

ROW 18 (WS, S/M ONLY): *P2, K8* twice, P2, *K8, P2* twice.

ROW 17 (RS, L/XL ONLY): Change to size 11 needles. P3, *K2, P8* twice, K2, *P8, K2*, twice, P3.

ROW 18 (WS, L/XL ONLY): K3, *P2, K8* twice, P2, *K8, P2* twice, K3.

Continue in pattern, increasing 1 st at each side every 6th row until there are 66 (74) sts. Work even until sleeve measures 21¾ in. long. BO in pattern. Wash and block the sleeves.

FELTING AND BLOCKING

The sweater body is too large to fit in a mesh lingerie bag. Place it in the washer, unbagged. Wash on the hot/cold cycle. Check the progress frequently and remove the sweater body when the desired amount of felting has taken place. Remove from the washer and rinse the sweater body in lukewarm water. Spin the excess moisture out. Pin and block the sweater body to the required measurements. Keep the edges straight. Allow to dry before removing pins.

BANDS AND ASSEMBLY

NOTE: You can use the sharp point of a smaller-size knitting needle (I used my cable needle) to pick up and knit stitches along the lightly felted edges of the jacket body. Or you can CO the required number of sts, knit the bands separately, and then sew them in place with matching sewing thread.

Bottom Band

Beginning at the lower left front opening corner, on the right side, with Emerald and size 11 needles, pick up and knit 102 (118, 134, 150) sts across the bottom of the jacket body. In general, pick up 1 st for each jacket body st, except across the cables. Only pick up 4 sts across each cable. Work 5 rows garter st (K each row). BO. Weave the loose ends in.

Cutting the Sleeve Steeks

Following the measurement illustration, fold the jacket body so that the cables at the shoulders line up (there will be a gap in the center front). Measure 10½ in. (10½ in., 11½ in., 11½ in.) down from the shoulder edge and cut for the sleeve openings. You can reinforce the cut edges with zigzag machine stitching, or you can whipstitch the edges with yarn to prevent raveling.

Sewing the Shoulder Seams

Matching the cables on the front and back shoulders, with yarn in a large-eye sharp needle, sew 6 in. (7 in., 8 in., 9 in.) in from the cut sleeve edge for the shoulder seam.

NECKLINE SHAPING

For all sizes, measure 3 in. down from the neckline and mark on either side of the jacket front. Mark an angle from that mark up to the edge of the shoulder seam on the front. Cut that portion of the front neckline out. Do not cut the back neckline area. You can reinforce the cut edges with zigzag machine stitching, or you can whipstitch the edges with yarn to prevent raveling.

Neck Band

With size 10 needles and Emerald, beginning at the upper right front neck edge, on the right side, pick up and K20 (22, 24, 26) sts from the neckline edge to the shoulder seam, pick up and K24 (26, 28, 30) sts evenly spaced across the back neckline, pick up and K20 (22, 24, 26) sts from the shoulder seam to the left front edge. (64, 70, 76, 82 sts)

Work 5 rows in garter st. BO. Weave the loose ends in.

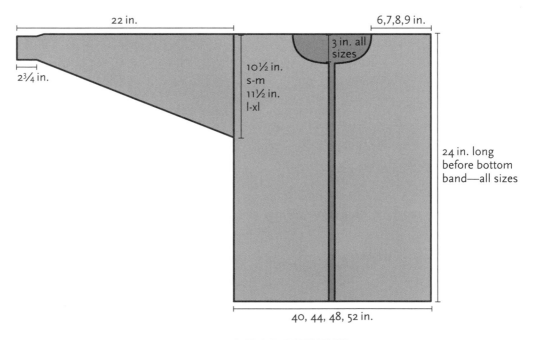

22 in.

6,7,8,9 in.

2¾ in.

3 in. all sizes

10½ in. s-m
11½ in. l-xl

24 in. long before bottom band—all sizes

40, 44, 48, 52 in.

CABLED EVERGREEN JACKET MEASUREMENTS

Left Front Band (all sizes)

With size 11 needles and Emerald, beginning at the left front neck edge, right side, pick up and knit 82 sts evenly spaced along the entire front opening. Work 5 rows in garter st. BO. Weave the loose ends in.

Right Front Buttonhole Band (all sizes)

With size 11 needles and Emerald, beginning at the lower right front opening, on the right side, pick up and knit 82 sts evenly spaced along the entire front opening. Work 2 rows in garter st.
BUTTONHOLE ROW: K5, K2 tog, YO, *K8, K2 tog, YO* 7 times, K5.
NEXT ROW: K, working each YO as a stitch.
NEXT ROW: K.
BO. Weave the loose ends in.

SLEEVE ASSEMBLY

With the right side out, and yarn threaded in a large-eye blunt needle, sew the sleeve seam. Pin the sleeve in the opening, easing as needed. With yarn threaded in a large-eye sharp needle, sew the sleeve in the armhole. Fold the cuffs up, if desired.

BUTTONS

With matching sewing thread, sew the buttons in place on the Left Front Band, opposite the buttonholes on the Buttonhole Band.

USING color

when you think of COLOR IN KNITTING, it follows that you would think of STRIPES.

There is nothing wrong with stripes— I LOVE STRIPES, especially the way they turned out in the Soft Stripes Hat on p. 88 and the tweedy color fade of the Men's Striped Slippers on p. 84. BUT THE EXPLORATION OF COLOR CAN GO FAR BEYOND SIMPLE OR EVEN COMPLEX STRIPING.

With only a little adaptation for knitted felt, intarsia is a breeze with the **Patchwork Intarsia Mittens** *(which coordinate with the* **Soft Stripes Hat***), the delightful* **Grazing Sheep Bag,** *and the charming* **Intarsia Sewing Kit.** *It takes a bit more adjustment to adapt Fair Isle knitting for felting, but we did it with the zesty* **Zigzag Hat,** *the* **Peppermint Stick Christmas Stocking,** *and the adorable* **Child-Size Gingham Vest.** ● *And color can be, well, just plain colorful, as with the* **I-Cord Belts and Headbands** *and the assortment of felted* **Autumn Harvest** *veggies.*

autumn harvest

Don't wait until autumn to decorate your table

with a brightly colored bowl of felted pumpkins, gourds, and squash. A fun project for any time of year, these 3D cuties are easy and small enough to make with leftover yarn.

Yarn:

Brown Sheep Lamb's Pride Worsted, 85% wool/15% mohair, 4 oz. (113 g), 190 yd., 1 skein each of #M22 Autumn Harvest, #M113 Oregano, #M155 Lemon Drop, #M14 Sunburst Gold, and #M188 Tiger Lily

Yarn Weight:

Worsted

Needles:

Size 9 (U.S.) dpn

Tools:

Large-eye blunt needle
Large-eye sharp needle

Notions:

Polyester fiberfill

Unfelted Gauge:

4 sts = 1 in., 6 rows = 1 in. in stockinette st

Number of Complete Washer Cycles to Felt as Shown:

(Adjust as necessary to achieve desired size.) 1

Sizes before Felting:

Small Pumpkin: 5 in. long (including stem), 11 in. around; Gourd: 8 in. long (including stem), 8 in. around; Acorn Squash: 5 in. long (including stem), 9 in. around; Butternut Squash: 7 in. long (including stem), 9 in. around; Large Pumpkin: 5 in. long (including stem), 13 in. around

Sizes after Felting:

(NOTE: Sizes can vary due to individual washer cycles. Finished items that are too large can be felted again. Finished items that are too small can be stretched while wet to add about 15 percent additional length and/or width.) Small Pumpkin: 3¾ in. long (including stem), 11 in. around; Gourd: 6½ in. long (including stem), 9 in. around; Acorn Squash: 5 in. long (including stem), 9 in. around; Butternut Squash: 5¾ in. long (including stem), 9½ in. around; Large Pumpkin: 4½ in. long (including stem), 14½ in. around

NOTE: These items are stuffed before felting. During washing the stuffing can shift, so the items often have a larger circumference after felting.

Number of Yarn Strands Used:

1 throughout

> **NEARLY ANY** orange, gold, yellow, or green wool yarn will be appropriate for felted, stuffed veggies.

SMALL PUMPKIN KNITTING INSTRUCTIONS

With size 9 needles and Oregano, CO 9 sts. Divide evenly on dpn and join.

RNDS 1–12: K.

RND 13: Change to Autumn Harvest, *K1, inc 1*, repeat around. (18 sts)

RND 14 AND ALL EVEN RNDS: K.

RND 15: *K1, inc 1*, repeat around. (36 sts)

RND 17: *K4, inc 1*, repeat around. (45 sts)

Work even for 3 in.

DECREASE RND 1: *K7, K2 tog*, repeat around. (36 sts)

DECREASE RND 2 AND ALL EVEN DECREASE RNDS: K.

DECREASE RND 3: *K2 tog*, repeat around. (18 sts)

Stuff pumpkin, including the stem, with polyester fiberfill. Add the stuffing smoothly and evenly, but do not overstuff (the stitches should not be stretched).

DECREASE RND 5: *K2 tog*, repeat around. (9 sts)

Add a little more stuffing if needed. Cut a 12-in. tail, and thread the tail in a large-eye blunt needle. Weave the tail through the remaining sts, tighten, and tie off. Weave the loose end in. Thread the CO tail in a large-eye blunt needle, and sew around the stem end. Tighten and tie off. Weave the loose end in. Cut an 18-in. length of yarn and thread it in a large-eye sharp needle. Anchor the yarn to the center bottom of the pumpkin, bring it up to the stem, sew through the base of the stem, and bring the yarn back down the other side of the pumpkin. Tighten to form the pumpkin sections. Tie off, and weave the loose ends in. Repeat a quarter turn from the first section (4 sections total).

LARGE PUMPKIN KNITTING INSTRUCTIONS

With size 9 needles and Oregano, CO 9 sts. Divide evenly on dpn and join.

RNDS 1–12: K.

RND 13: Change to Tiger Lily. *K1, inc 1*, repeat around. (18 sts)

RND 14 AND ALL EVEN RNDS: K.

RND 15: *K1, inc 1*, repeat around. (36 sts)

RND 17: *K4, inc 1*, repeat around. (45 sts)

RND 19: *K5, inc 1*, repeat around. (54 sts)

Work even for 3½ in.

DECREASE RND 1: *K7, K2 tog*, repeat around. (48 sts)

DECREASE RND 2 AND ALL EVEN DECREASE RNDS: K.

DECREASE RND 3: *K6, K2 tog*, repeat around. (36 sts)

DECREASE RND 5: *K2 tog*, repeat around. (18 sts)

Stuff pumpkin, including the stem, with polyester fiberfill. Add the stuffing smoothly and evenly, but do not overstuff (the stitches should not be stretched).

DECREASE RND 7: *K2 tog*, repeat around. (9 sts)
Add a little more stuffing if needed. Cut a 12-in. tail,
and thread the tail in a large-eye blunt needle. Weave
the tail through the remaining sts, tighten, and tie off.
Weave the loose end in. Thread the CO tail in a large-eye
blunt needle, and sew around the stem end. Tighten
and tie off. Weave the loose end in. Cut an 18-in. length
of yarn and thread in a large-eye sharp needle. Anchor
the yarn to the center bottom of the pumpkin, bring it
up to the stem, sew through the base of the stem, and
bring the yarn back down the other side of the pumpkin.
Tighten to form the pumpkin sections. Tie off, and
weave the loose ends in. Repeat twice more, evenly
spaced around the pumpkin (6 sections total).

GOURD
KNITTING
INSTRUCTIONS

With size 9 needles and Oregano, CO 9 sts. Divide
evenly on dpn and join.

RNDS 1–12: K.

RND 13: Change to Lemon Drop. K.

RND 14: K.

RND 15: *K1, inc 1*, repeat around. (18 sts)
Work even for 2 in.

NEXT RND: *K1, inc 1*, repeat around. (36 sts)
Work even for 3 in.

DECREASE RND 1: *K4, K2 tog*, repeat around. (24 sts)

DECREASE RND 2: K.

Stuff gourd, including the stem, with polyester fiberfill.
Add the stuffing smoothly and evenly, but do not
overstuff (the stitches should not be stretched).

DECREASE RND 3: *K4, K2 tog*, repeat around. (12 sts)

DECREASE RND 4: *K2 tog*, repeat around. (6 sts).
Add a little more stuffing if needed. Cut a 12-in. tail, and
thread the tail in a large-eye blunt needle. Weave the tail
through the remaining sts, tighten, and tie off. Weave
the loose end in. Thread the CO tail in a large-eye blunt
needle, and sew around the stem end. Tighten and tie
off. Weave the loose end in.

ACORN SQUASH
KNITTING
INSTRUCTIONS

Work and stuff as for Small Pumpkin, using Oregano
throughout. Make sections with Lemon Drop yarn as for
Large Pumpkin (6 sections total).

BUTTERNUT SQUASH
KNITTING
INSTRUCTIONS

With size 9 needles and Oregano, CO 9 sts. Divide
evenly on dpn and join.

RNDS 1–12: K.

RND 13: Change to Sunburst Gold. K.

RND 14: K.

RND 15: *K1, inc 1*, repeat around. (18 sts)
Work even for 2 in.

NEXT RND: *K1, inc 1*, repeat around. (36 sts)

NEXT RND: K.

NEXT RND: *K4, inc 1*, repeat around. (45 sts)
Work even for 3 in.

DECREASE RND 1: *K5, K2 tog*, repeat around. (36 sts)
DECREASE RND 2 AND ALL EVEN DECREASE RNDS: K.
DECREASE RND 3: *K2 tog*, repeat around. (18 sts)
Stuff Butternut Squash, including the stem, with polyester fiberfill. Add the stuffing smoothly and evenly, but do not overstuff (the stitches should not be stretched).

DECREASE RND 5: *K2 tog*, repeat around. (9 sts)
Add a little more stuffing if needed. Cut a 12-in. tail, and thread the tail in a large-eye blunt needle. Weave the tail through the remaining sts, tighten, and tie off. Weave the loose end in. Thread the CO tail in a large-eye blunt needle, and sew around the stem end. Tighten and tie off. Weave the loose end in. Cut an 18-in. length of yarn and thread it in a large-eye sharp needle. Anchor the yarn at the center bottom of the Butternut Squash, and bring the yarn up through the polyester fiberfill and out at the point where the squash flares from the neck. Bring the yarn back through the polyester fiberfill and back out the center bottom and tighten and tie the yarn. Repeat several times around the Butternut Squash. Weave all loose ends in.

FELTING

Place 2 or 3 items (do not overcrowd) in a mesh zippered lingerie bag and wash on the hot/cold cycle. Check the progress frequently and remove them when desired amount of felting has taken place. Pull the pieces into shape, forming the Small Pumpkin, Large Pumpkin, and Butternut Squash to be squat and round, forming the

Gourd to be long and smooth, and forming the Acorn Squash to be oval shaped. Form the Gourd and Squash stems into a curve. Allow items to dry. It might take several days for the stuffing to dry completely.

I-Cord Belts & Headbands:
A Good Leftover Yarn Project

Dress up every outfit with quick-to-knit

*I-cord belts and matching headbands. This braided headband and these skinny belts
are made from fingering-weight sock yarn and Knit Picks Palette™, but you can knit
and felt I-cord from any leftover yarn for these stylish accessories.*

Yarn:

TIE BELT: Variegated sock yarn,
100% Merino wool, 50 g, 220 yd.,
#23842 Spring Prairie, 1 skein
Knit Picks Palette, 100% Peruvian
wool, 50 g, 231 yd., #23711 Lemon,
#23719 Purple, 1 skein each

D-RING BELT: Variegated sock yarn,
#23846 Rocky Mountain Dusk,
1 skein

HEADBAND: Variegated sock yarn,
1 #23845 Redwood Forest, 1 skein
Knit Picks Palette, #23737 Bark,
1 skein

Yarn Weight:
Fingering

Needles:
Size 4 (U.S.) dpn

Tools:
Large-eye blunt needle
Sewing needle
Clothespin

Notions:
Matching thread
2 D-rings

Sizes:
One size fits all

Unfelted Gauge:
Gauge is not important.

Number of Complete Washer

Cycles to Felt as Shown:
(Adjust as necessary to achieve
desired size.) 1

Sizes before Felting:
Each I-cord approx 6 ft. to 8 ft. long

Sizes after Felting:
(NOTE: Sizes can vary due to
individual washer cycles. Finished
items that are too large can be
felted again. Finished items that
are too small can be stretched
while wet to add about 15 percent
additional length and/or width.)
Each I-cord approx 4 ft. to 6 ft. long

Number of Yarn Strands Used:
1 throughout

IF YOU WANT TO USE HEAVIER YARNS TO MAKE I-CORD BELTS AND HEADBANDS, use larger needles to knit the I-cords: size 6 (U.S.) with sport-weight yarn, size 8 (U.S.) with DK-weight yarn, size 9 (U.S.) with worsted-weight yarn, size 11 (U.S.) with bulky-weight yarn. Each belt/headband uses approximately 1 oz. of assorted colors of fingering-weight yarn. You will need more yardage of the heavier yarns for these projects. When using heavier yarns, only cast on 3 stitches.

KNITTING INSTRUCTIONS

NOTE: General instructions for knitting and felting I-cord are given here. Specific directions for each project follow.

CO 4 sts.

ROW 1: K across. Do not turn.

ROW 2: Slide the sts to the right side of the needle, bring the yarn around behind the work, and tighten. K across.

Rep Row 2 until I-cord is the desired length (8 ft. for the belts, 6 ft. for the headband).

LAST ROW: Cut a 6-in. tail. Thread the tail in a large-eye needle and sew through all 4 loops. Tighten and tie off. Weave the end in on the inside of the I-cord. Weave the other end in on the inside of the I-cord.

FELTING

Place I-cords in a mesh zippered lingerie bag and wash on the hot/cold cycle. Check the progress frequently and remove them when the desired amount of felting has taken place. Remove I-cords from the lingerie bag and pull them straight. Allow them to dry.

NOTE: Braided, felted I-cords are fairly elastic, so the finished items can be stretched to fit, if needed.

Tassel Belt

Knit one 8-ft. I-cord each from Spring Prairie, Lemon, and Purple. Felt them and allow them to dry.

1. Line all 3 I-cords up, with the ends even. Measure 12 in. from the end and hold in place with a clothespin.
2. With matching sewing thread, sew the 3 I-cords together at the 12-in. mark.
3. Braid the I-cords together for 36 in. (or for desired length). Hold the braided I-cords in place with a clothespin. With matching sewing thread, sew the 3 I-cords together at the end of the braiding.
4. Measure 12 in. from the sewing, and cut the I-cords. Tie a small knot in the end of each I-cord.

Tassel Headband

Knit two 6-ft. I-cords from Redwood Forest and one 6-ft. I-cord from Bark. Felt them and allow them to dry.

1. Line all 3 I-cords up, with the ends even. Measure 2 in. from the end and hold in place with a clothespin.
2. Sew and braid 24 in. (or desired length).
3. Sew as for the Tassel Belt. Trim the remaining I-cords to 2 in.

D-Ring Belt

Knit three 8-ft. I-cords from Rocky Mountain Dusk. Felt them and allow them to dry.

1. Line all 3 I-cords up, with the ends even. With matching sewing thread, sew the ends together.
2. Braid the strands together for 44 in. (or for desired length). Place a clothespin at the end of the braiding, and with matching sewing thread, sew the strands together at the end of the braiding.
3. Measure and cut the I-cords 2 in. from the sewing.
4. Fold the 2-in. I-cord trimmed ends over the flat side of one D-ring. Sew them down on the wrong side of the belt.
5. Cut three 2-in. pieces from the leftover I-cord. Line them up and sew them together at one end. Tack that end 1½ in. from the first D-ring, on the right side of the belt.
6. Thread the tacked I-cord ends over the second D-ring and sew them in place on the right side of the belt.
7. Sew the strands around both D-rings securely.

men's striped slippers

Keep his feet toasty warm in these tweedy

striped slippers. You can add nonskid or leather bottoms if desired.

Yarn:
Knit Picks Shamrock,™ 100%
Peruvian wool, 50 g, 82 yd ,
#23972 Doyle, 4 balls
Knit Picks Wool of the Andes,
100% Peruvian wool, 50 g, 110 yd.,
#23420 Coal, 2 balls; #23429
Snickerdoodle, #23422 Winter
Night, and #24068 Cerulean,
1 ball each

Yarn Weight:
Worsted

Needles:
Size 11 (U.S.) dpn, 10 in.

Tools:
Large-eye blunt needle

Sizes:
Men's Small, shoe sizes 9–10
(Medium, shoe sizes 10½–11;
Large, shoe sizes 12–13)

Unfelted Gauge:
3 sts = 1 in., 4 rnds = 1 in. in
stockinette st

**Number of Complete Washer
Cycles to Felt as Shown:**
(Adjust as necessary to achieve
desired size.) 2

Sizes before Felting:
15 in. (17 in., 19 in.) long, 8 in.
wide, lying flat (all sizes)

Sizes after Felting:
(NOTE: Sizes can vary due to
individual washer cycles. Finished
items that are too large can be
felted again. Finished items that
are too small can be stretched
while wet to add about 15 percent
additional length and/or width.)
9½ in. (10½ in., 11½ in.) long,
5½ in. wide, lying flat (all sizes)

Number of Yarn Strands Used:
2 throughout

KNITTING INSTRUCTIONS

Slippers (make 2)

With 1 strand of Doyle and 1 strand of Coal held together, CO 48 sts. Divide evenly on 3 dpn, making sure the stitches are not twisted, and join.

RND 1: K.

DIVIDE FOR HEEL: K24. Place the remaining sts on a single needle. Work on the first 24 sts for the heel, turn, and begin work on the wrong side.

HEEL FLAP ROW 1: Sl 1, P across, turn.

HEEL FLAP ROW 2: Sl 1, K across, turn.

Work a total of 15 Heel Flap rows, ending with a purl row, turn.

HEEL TURNING ROW 1: Sl 1, K13, K2 tog, K1, turn.

HEEL TURNING ROW 2: Sl 1, P5, P2 tog, P1, turn.

HEEL TURNING ROW 3: Sl 1, K6, K2 tog, K1, turn.

Continue in this way, working 1 more st before the decrease (either *K2 tog, K1, turn*, or *P2 tog, P1, turn*) on each row. Continue until you have worked across the entire set of Heel sts. End with a purl row.

GUSSET RND 1: Sl 1, K half of the heel sts. These sts are now Needle #3. Start a new needle and K the remaining heel sts. Pick up and knit 12 sts along the flap. These sts are now Needle #1. K across Needle #2. Pick up and knit 12 sts along the flap, K the remaining sts on Needle #3.

GUSSET RND 2: K to within 2 sts of the end of Needle #1, K2 tog; K across Needle #2; on Needle #3, K2 tog, K the remaining sts.

GUSSET RND 3 AND ALL ODD GUSSET RNDS: K. Repeat Gusset Rnds 2–3 until there are 12 sts left on Needles #1 and #3. The stitch number on Needle #2 does not change. Redistribute the sts evenly on the 3 needles.

At the same time, work the stripes in the following progression from the beginning of the Gusset: 8 rnds Doyle and Coal, 8 rnds Doyle and Winter Night, 8 rnds Doyle and Cerulean, 8 rnds Doyle and Snickerdoodle. Work even, changing colors as directed, until the slipper measures 8¾ in. (10¾ in., 12¾ in.) from the beginning of the gusset sts.

TOE DECREASE RND 1: *K6, K2 tog*, repeat around.

TOE DECREASE RND 2 AND ALL EVEN TOE DECREASE RNDS: K.

TOE DECREASE RND 3: *K5, K2 tog*, repeat around.

TOE DECREASE RND 5: *K4, K2 tog*, repeat around.

TOE DECREASE RND 7: *K3, K2 tog*, repeat around.

TOE DECREASE RND 9: *K2, K2 tog*, repeat around.

TOE DECREASE RND 11: *K1, K2 tog*, repeat around.

Cut yarns, leaving a 12-in. tail. Thread tail yarns in a large-eye needle and weave through the remaining sts. Tighten and tie off on the inside of the slipper. Weave in the tails at the foot opening. Trim the remaining tails to within 1 in. of the fabric inside the slipper. Trim the felted ends flush with the fabric after felting.

FELTING

Place the slippers in a mesh zippered lingerie bag and wash on the hot/cold cycle. Check the progress frequently and remove the slippers when the desired amount of felting has taken place. Remove from the lingerie bag and the shape the slippers by hand. If the foot opening feels tight, stretch it while the slipper is still wet. You can stuff the foot with plastic bags to help the slipper hold its shape while drying. Allow the slippers to dry.

NOTE: If the foot opening is too tight after stretching, you can trim the upper fabric with scissors. Cut only about ¼ in. from the opening edge at a time until the slippers slide on the feet easily.

soft stripes hat

This soft, simple striped hat coordinates

with the Patchwork Intarsia Mittens and looks great on a guy or a gal.

Yarn:
Knit Picks Merino Style™, 100% Merino wool, 50 g, 123 yd., 1 skein each of #23443 Rhubarb, #23446 Cornflower, #23458 Dusk, #23450 Fog, and #23444 Vanilla

Yarn Weight:
DK

Needles:
Size 8 (U.S.) circular, 16 in.
Size 8 (U.S.) dpn

Tools:
1 stitch marker
Large-eye blunt needle

Sizes:
Child (Adult)

Unfelted Gauge:
4.5 sts = 1 in., 6 rows = 1 in. in stockinette st

Number of Complete Washer Cycles to Felt as Shown:
(Adjust as necessary to achieve desired size.) Less than 1. Remove hat after 8 minutes of agitation, or when desired amount of felting has occurred.

Sizes before Felting:
Approx 11 in. (12 in.) wide lying flat, approx 8½ in. (10½ in.) long

Sizes after Felting:
(NOTE: Sizes can vary due to individual washer cycles. Finished items that are too large can be felted again. Finished items that are too small can be stretched while wet to add about 15 percent additional length and/or width.) Approx 10 in. (11 in.) wide lying flat, 7 in. (8 in.) long

Number of Yarn Strands Used:
1 throughout

KNITTING INSTRUCTIONS

With Vanilla and size 8 circular needle, CO 100 (110) sts. Place stitch marker to mark the beginning of the rnd, make sure that the stitches are not twisted, and join.

STRIPE PATTERN: Work striped bands consisting of 11 rnds of each color in the following order: Rhubarb, Cornflower, Dusk, Fog.

ADULT SIZE ONLY: Work an additional band of Vanilla. (44, 55 rnds total)

HAT DECREASE RND (ADULT SIZE ONLY; USE CORNFLOWER): *K9, K2 tog*, repeat around. (100 sts remain)

HAT DECREASE RND 1, ALL SIZES (FOR CHILD SIZE USE VANILLA; FOR ADULT SIZE USE CORNFLOWER): *K8, K2tog*, repeat around. (90 sts remain)

HAT DECREASE RND 2 AND ALL EVEN RNDS: K.

HAT DECREASE RND 3: *K7, K2 tog*, repeat around. (80 sts remain)

HAT DECREASE RND 5: *K6, K2 tog*, repeat around. (70 sts remain)

HAT DECREASE RND 7: *K5, K2 tog*, repeat around. (60 sts remain)

HAT DECREASE RND 9: *K4, K2 tog*, repeat around. (50 sts remain)

HAT DECREASE RND 11: *K3, K2 tog*, repeat around. (40 sts remain)

HAT DECREASE RND 13: *K2, K2 tog*, repeat around. (30 sts remain)

HAT DECREASE RND 15: *K1, K2 tog*, repeat around. (20 sts remain)

HAT DECREASE RND 17: *K2 tog*, repeat around. (10 sts remain)

Cut a tail 12 in. long. Thread the tail in a large-eye needle. Weave the tail through the remaining sts, tighten, and tie off. Weave the tail in on the inside of the hat. Weave the CO tail in at the lower edge of the hat. Trim the remaining tails to 1 in.

FELTING

Place hat in a mesh zippered lingerie bag and wash on the hot/cold cycle. Check the progress frequently and remove the hat when the desired amount of felting has taken place. Rinse in warm water and spin the excess moisture out. Pull the hat into shape, and allow to dry. Place hat on a foam head or stuff with plastic bags to hold shape, if desired. After hat has dried, trim the tails flush with the fabric.

patchwork intarsia mittens

These colorful intarsia mittens are a snap to knit—

work them flat on two needles and then sew the side and thumb seams before felting.

Yarn:
Knit Picks Merino Style, 100% Merino wool, 50 g, 123 yd., 1 skein each of #23443 Rhubarb, #23446 Cornflower, #23458 Dusk, #23450 Fog, and #23444 Vanilla

Yarn Weight:
DK

Needles:
Size 8 (U.S.) straight, 10 in.

Tools:
4 (5) small bobbins (optional)
Small stitch holder (or large safety pin)
2 stitch markers
Large-eye blunt needle

Sizes:
Child (Adult)

Unfelted Gauge:
4.5 sts = 1 in., 6 rows = 1 in. in stockinette st

Number of Complete Washer Cycles to Felt as Shown:
(Adjust as necessary to achieve desired size.) Less than 1. Remove mittens after 8 minutes of agitation, or when desired amount of felting has occurred.

Sizes before Felting:
With side seam unsewn, approx 9 in. (11 in.) wide, 10½ in. (12½ in.) long

Sizes after Felting:
(NOTE: Sizes can vary due to individual washer cycles. Finished items that are too large can be felted again. Finished items that are too small can be stretched while wet to add about 15 percent additional length and/or width.)
With side seam sewn: 4 in. (4½ in.) wide, 8¼ in. (10 in. long)

Number of Yarn Strands Used:
1 throughout

KNITTING INSTRUCTIONS

NOTE: *When changing colors across the row, always loop the new color around the old color on the wrong side before proceeding. Wind the yarns on small bobbins. Each color section takes approximately 8 ft. 6 in. of yarn.*

Left Mitten

With Vanilla and size 8 needles, CO 40 (50) sts.

ROW 1: Follow chart, beginning where indicated for the Child and Adult sizes. Tie on new colors as indicated, K across.

ROW 2: P, following chart.

Follow chart for 30 rows total (all sizes).

THUMB GUSSET ROW 1: Work according to chart for 20 (25) sts. Place marker. Pick up and knit 2 sts from the row below, place marker, work across according to chart. (2 sts inc)

THUMB GUSSET ROW 2 (AND ALL WS THUMB GUSSET ROWS): P, following chart.

THUMB GUSSET ROW 3: Work according to chart to the marker, slide the marker, inc 1, K to marker, inc 1, move marker, work across, following chart. (2 sts inc)

Repeat Thumb Gusset Rows 2–3 until 10 (12) sts are between the markers, changing colors as needed according to the chart. End with a purl row.

Work 4 rows even, ending with a purl row.

HAND ROW 1: Work according to chart, place the 10 (12) thumb gusset sts on a stitch holder, finish working row according to chart.

Work even, following chart, for 12 (26) rows. End with a purl row.

DECREASE ROW 1: *K8, K2 tog*, repeat across.

NOTE: *Decreases will land in the middles of the color squares on the Child size, and at the edge of the color squares for the Adult size.* (36, 45 sts remain)

DECREASE ROW 2 AND ALL EVEN DECREASE ROWS: P.

DECREASE ROW 3: *K7, K2 tog*, repeat across.
(32, 40 sts remain)

DECREASE ROW 5: *K6, K2 tog*, repeat across.
(28, 35 sts remain)

DECREASE ROW 7: *K5, K2 tog*, repeat across.
(24, 30 sts remain)

DECREASE ROW 9: *K4, K2 tog*, repeat across.
(20, 25 sts remain)

DECREASE ROW 11: *K3, K2 tog*, repeat across.
(16, 20 sts remain)

Work 1 row even.

BO all sts, using the proper color yarn for each section. Cut yarn, leaving a 15-in. tail. Weave tail through last loop and tighten.

Thumb

Place thumb sts on needle.

ROW 1: With proper color yarn, CO 1, K across, CO 1.
(2 sts inc—12, 14 sts total)

ROW 2: P.

Work even for a total of 8 (10) rows.

THUMB DECREASE ROW 1: *K2 tog*, repeat across.

THUMB DECREASE ROW 2: *P2 tog*, repeat across.

Adult size only: end with P1.

BO all sts. Cut a 10-in. tail. Weave tail through last loop and tighten.

Weave in loose ends along the bottom edge of the mitten. Trim all other color-change tails and loose ends to about 1 in. long. Do not trim the 15-in. and 10-in. tails.

Right Mitten

Work as for Left Mitten, but reverse the color progression.

ASSEMBLY

1. Before felting, fold the mitten in half, right side out. With the 15-in. tail threaded in a large-eye needle, sew the side seam from the upper BO edge down to the cuff edge, lining the color squares up as you sew.
2. Fold the thumb in half, right side out. With the 10-in. tail threaded in a large-eye needle, sew the thumb side seam from the upper BO edge down to the hand. Secure the thumb to the hand in the gap with a couple of stitches. Tie the yarn off on the inside of the mitten.

FELTING

Place mittens in a mesh zippered lingerie bag and wash on the hot/cold cycle. Check the progress frequently and remove the mittens when the desired amount of felting has taken place. Rinse in warm water and spin the excess moisture out. Pull the mittens into shape, and allow to dry flat.

NOTE: After felting and drying, turn the mittens inside out and trim the felted color-change tail ends flush with the fabric.

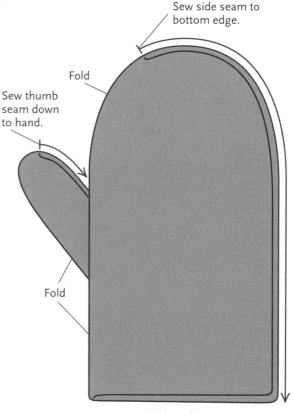

Sew side seam to bottom edge.

Fold

Sew thumb seam down to hand.

Fold

Right side out

PATCHWORK INTARSIA MITTENS SEWING GUIDE

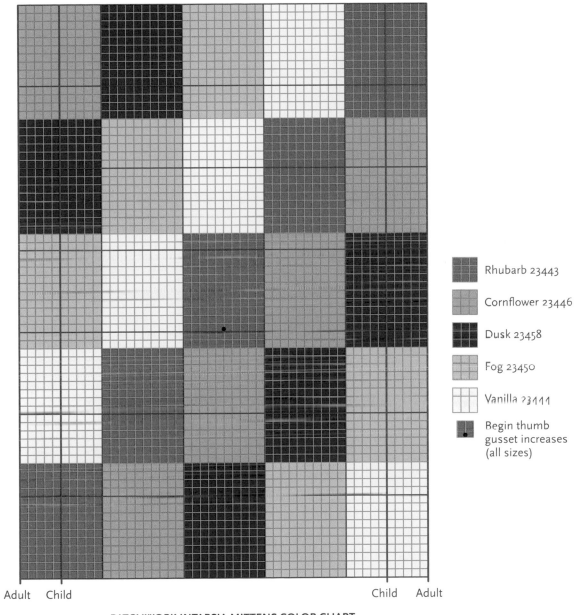

Rhubarb 23443

Cornflower 23446

Dusk 23458

Fog 23450

Vanilla 23111

Begin thumb
gusset increases
(all sizes)

Adult   Child   Child   Adult

PATCHWORK INTARSIA MITTENS COLOR CHART

intarsia sewing kit

Practice your intarsia knitting with this lovely

and practical little sewing kit. The bright colors and geometric shapes make following the chart a snap. And since only small amounts of each color are used, this is a good project for leftover yarns.

Yarn:
Knit Picks Merino Style, 100% Merino wool, 50 g, 123 yd., 1 skein each of #23463 Moss, #23453 Crocus, #23459 Frost, and #23460 Nutmeg

Yarn Weight:
DK

Needles:
Size 9 (U.S.) straight, 10 in.

Tools:
Yarn bobbins (optional)
Large-eye blunt needle
Large-eye sharp needle
Sewing needle

Notions:
7-in. by 6-in. purchased lightweight wool felt fabric, off white
Small sewing kit (or small scissors, needles, pins, buttons, thread)
White elastic cord
2 glass beads
Off-white sewing thread

Unfelted Gauge:
Approx 4.5 sts = 1 in., 6 rows = 1 in. in stockinette st

Number of Complete Washer Cycles to Felt as Shown:
(Adjust as necessary to achieve desired size.) Less than 1. Agitate for 5 minutes, then remove and rinse in lukewarm water.

Size before Felting:
8 in. wide, 7 in. tall

Size after Felting:
7 in. wide, 5¼ in. tall

Finished Dimensions:
(Assembled and closed) 3½ in. wide, 5 in. tall

Number of Yarn Strands Used:
1 throughout

KNITTING INSTRUCTIONS

With size 9 needles and Moss, CO 36.

ROW 1: K.

Follow the chart, from bottom to top, changing colors as directed, working in stockinette st throughout.

LAST ROW: Tie off all colors except Moss. Work 1 row in stockinette st.

BO all stitches.

Weave in the CO and BO tails. Tighten all of the loose ends from the color changes and trim closely on the back of work.

FELTING

Place the piece in a mesh zippered lingerie bag and wash on the hot/cold cycle. Check the progress frequently and remove the piece when the desired amount of felting has taken place. Rinse in lukewarm water and spin to remove excess moisture. Trim the felted ends flush with the fabric on the wrong side of the piece. Pull the piece into shape, making all edges straight. Allow piece to dry.

ASSEMBLY

Bead Closure

Select 1 glass bead. Thread white elastic cord in a large-eye sharp needle. Lay the felted fabric right side up. Bring the elastic cord from the wrong side of the fabric, at the center, ½ in. in from the right edge. Thread the cord through the bead. Tie the cord together, leaving some slack in the elastic between the bead and the knot, and sew the remainder of the cord back through to the wrong side of the fabric. Pull the cord ends tightly and tie in a secure knot. Repeat with the other bead on the left side, but anchor the bead on the wrong side of the fabric.

Anchoring the Sewing Supplies

Trim the purchased wool felt fabric liner ¼ in. smaller all around than the felted intarsia cover. Place the assorted sewing kit pieces (scissors, thread, pins, etc.) on the felt lining, making sure that none are on the middle crease. Use white elastic cord threaded in a large-eye sharp needle and sew small loops of elastic over each piece. Tighten and tie off the elastic cord on the wrong side of the felt lining. Attach safety pins directly to the liner.

THE COLOR SECTIONS in this project are all small, using only about 1 yd. of yarn apiece. You may wind the yarn colors on small bobbins (one bobbin for each color section in each row, though you may have more than one bobbin per color per row), or you can just let the yarn hang loose on the wrong side of the work. When you change colors, wrap the new color around the old color to avoid holes in the work.

Sewing the Lining

With the sewing supplies anchored by elastic on the liner, whipstitch the liner to the wrong side of the felted fabric using off-white sewing thread. To close the case, fold the kit in half and bring the back bead elastic up and over the front bead.

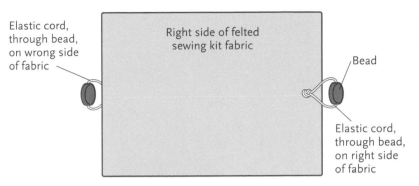

Elastic cord, through bead, on wrong side of fabric

Right side of felted sewing kit fabric

Bead

Elastic cord, through bead, on right side of fabric

INTARSIA SEWING KIT ASSEMBLY

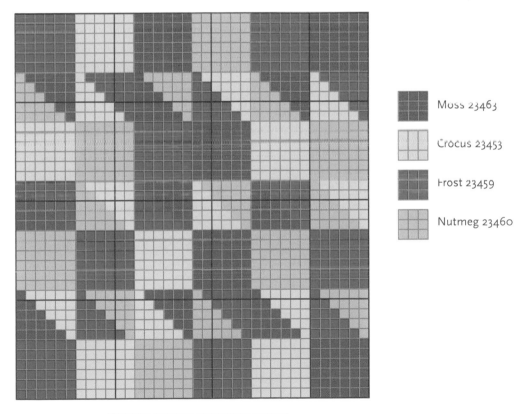

INTARSIA SEWING KIT COLOR CHART

Moss 23463

Crocus 23453

Frost 23459

Nutmeg 23460

grazing sheep bag

This adorable bag with sheep grazing on a hillside

is knit flat and seamed before felting. Sew a simple fabric lining for the bag, attach purchased handles, and you and your sheep are ready to carry your knitting projects wherever you go.

Yarn:
Knit Picks Wool of the Andes, 100% Peruvian wool, 50 g, 100 yd., #23766 Avocado, 2 skeins; #23767 Asparagus, #23439 Grass, #23434 Stream, #24068 Cerulean, #23420 Coal, and #23432 Cloud, 1 skein each

Yarn Weight:
Worsted

Needles:
Size 9 (U.S.) straight, 10 in.

Tools:
2 stitch markers
Yarn bobbins (optional)
Large-eye blunt needle
Sewing needle

Notions:
18-in. by 20-in. lightweight fabric for lining

Matching sewing thread
1 pair wooden bag handles

Unfelted Gauge:
5 sts = 1 in., 6 rows = 1 in. in stockinette st

Number of Complete Washer Cycles to Felt as Shown:
(Adjust as necessary to achieve desired size.) 1

Size before Felting:
After sewing back and bottom seams: 10 in. wide, 17¼ in. long

Size after Felting:
(NOTE: Sizes can vary due to individual washer cycles. Finished items that are too large can be felted again. Finished items that are too small can be stretched while wet to add about 15 percent additional length and/or width.) Approx 9 in. wide, 12 in. long

Number of Yarn Strands Used:
1 throughout

NOTE. Do not strand the colors more than 3 or 4 stitches in this piece because the strands will shrink more than the knitted fabric during felting. Tie on new yarn for each color section (for example, for each sheep leg, and before and after each sheep body). Wind the yarn on bobbins or, if the sections are small, just let the yarn hang on the back of the work. When changing colors in a row, wrap the new color under and around the old color before working the next stitch.

KNITTING INSTRUCTIONS

With size 9 needles and Avocado, CO 100 sts. Beginning at the lower right edge of the chart, working in stockinette st throughout, knit the chart in the colors as shown. Place markers 25 sts from either end. The center 50 sts are the front of the bag. When you have worked the entire chart, BO with Cerulean.

With matching yarns threaded in a large-eye needle, sew the center back seam. Lay the bag flat with the front centered, and use Avocado threaded in a large-eye needle to sew the bottom seam.

FELTING

Place the bag in a mesh zippered lingerie bag and wash on the hot/cold cycle. Check the progress frequently and remove the bag when the desired amount of felting has taken place. Remove the bag from the lingerie bag and smooth it into shape, making all of the edges straight. Allow bag to dry. After the bag is felted, turn it inside out and trim all of the felted tails flush with the fabric.

ASSEMBLY

1. Fold the lining fabric in half, right side in. Measure the width of the dried, felted bag and add ½ in. Mark that measurement from the fabric fold and cut the fabric.
2. Measure the length of the bag. Add 2 in. to that measurement. Mark that measurement along the upper portion of the fabric and cut the fabric.
3. With the right side in, and using matching thread, hand- or machine-stitch ¼ in. in from the outer edge of the bag lining. Trim the corner, but do not turn the lining right side out.
4. Fold the upper edge out and down 2½ in., and stitch in place.
5. Open the bag and place the lining inside, with the lining side seam matching the side of the bag. With matching sewing thread, hand- or machine-stitch the lining in place, ½ in. below the felted upper opening.
6. Using Cerulean, sew the handles in place.

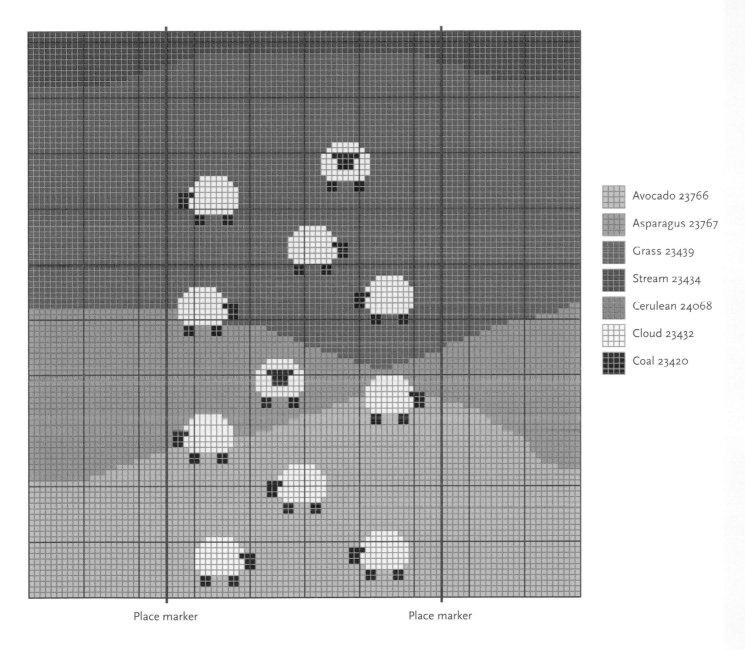

Place marker   Place marker

Avocado 23766
Asparagus 23767
Grass 23439
Stream 23434
Cerulean 24068
Cloud 23432
Coal 23420

GRAZING SHEEP COLOR CHART

zigzag hat

If you're nervous about Fair Isle and stranded

knitting, try this easy Zigzag Hat, made by knitting a simple tube and sewing the top together. The chart is simple to follow, and the stylish crown is easy to shape.

Yarn:
Cascade 220 Quatro, 100% Peruvian highland wool, 100 g, 220 yd., 1 skein each of #5017 (purple), #5010 (yellow), #5011 (orange)

Yarn Weight:
Worsted

Needles:
Size 9 (U.S.) circular, 16 in.

Tools:
Large-eye blunt needle

Sizes:
Child (Adult)

Unfelted Gauge:
5 sts = 1 in., 5 rnds = 1 in. in stockinette st

Number of Complete Washer Cycles to Felt as Shown:
(Adjust as necessary to achieve desired size.) 1

Sizes before Felting:
12 in. (13 in.) wide, lying flat; 10 in. (12 in.) long

Sizes after Felting:
(NOTE: Sizes can vary due to individual washer cycles. Finished items that are too large can be felted again. Finished items that are too small can be stretched while wet to add about 15 percent additional length and/or width.) Approx 9½ in. (10½ in.) wide lying flat; 6½ in. (8 in.) tall

Number of Yarn Strands Used:
1 throughout

AS WITH ALL FAIR ISLE KNITTING, felted or unfelted, strand the unused yarns loosely and evenly on the wrong side of the work. Leave at least a 3-in. tail when tying on new yarns.

KNITTING INSTRUCTIONS

With size 9 (U.S.) circular needle, and purple and yellow, CO 136 (148) sts, alternating 2 sts purple and 2 sts yellow as you CO.

K each rnd, following the chart and repeating borders, until hat measures 10 in. (12 in.) long. BO, alternating colors as per the chart.

Weave in the loose ends on the upper and lower edges.

ASSEMBLY

1. Lay the unfelted hat flat. Find and mark the top center edge. Mark the top side center points.
2. Pin the top center points together. Bring the top side center points to the top center point and pin in place. The top will now resemble an X.
3. With yarn threaded in a large-eye needle (either color from the topmost border), sew the top points. Weave the loose ends in on the inside of the hat.

FELTING

Place hat in a mesh zippered lingerie bag and wash on the hot/cold cycle. Check the progress frequently and remove the hat when the desired amount of felting has taken place. Remove the hat from the lingerie bag and pull it into shape, making the upper X straight, and the bottom even. If the hat is too tight after one full washer cycle, stretch the bottom edge. If it is too loose, felt

another cycle. Do the shaping while the hat is still wet. You can dry the hat on a mannequin head form, or stuff it with plastic bags to hold the shape, if desired.

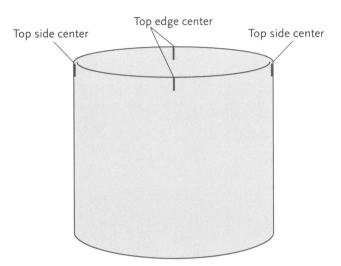

ZIGZAG HAT SEWING GUIDE 1

ZIGZAG HAT SEWING GUIDE 2

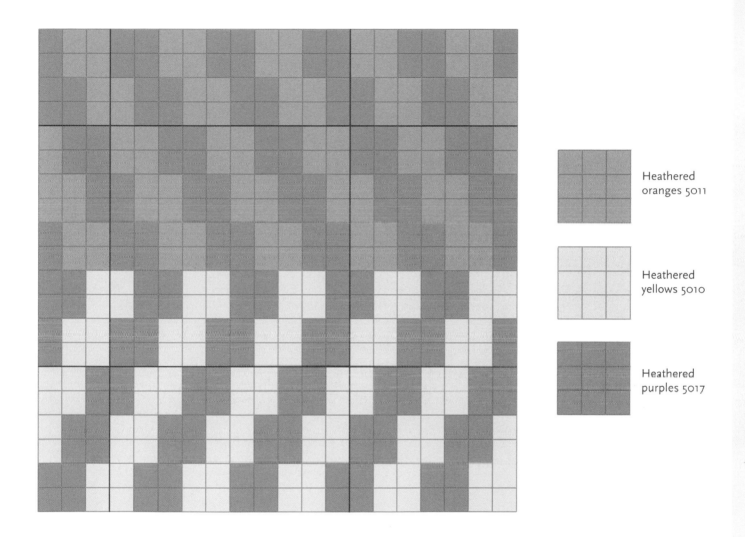

Heathered
oranges 5011

Heathered
yellows 5010

Heathered
purples 5017

ZIGZAG HAT COLOR CHART

peppermint stick christmas stocking

Start knitting now, and by next holiday season

you can fill this yummy Fair Isle Peppermint Stick Christmas Stocking with delicious holiday goodies. Or use a different color scheme, and hang it year-round.

Yarn:
Knit Picks Wool of the Andes, 100% Peruvian wool, 50 g, 110 yd., #23420 Coal, 2 skeins; #23425 Cranberry, #23431 Tomato, #24077 Dove Heather, 1 skein each Knit Picks Bare—Peruvian Wool Worsted Weight, 100% Peruvian wool, 100 g, 220 yd., #23417 Natural, 1 skein

Yarn Weight:
Worsted

Needles:
Size 9 (U.S.) dpn, 10 in.

Tools:
Large-eye blunt needle
Medium stitch holder (optional)
Sewing needle

Notions:
Matching thread

Unfelted Gauge:
Approx 5.5 **sts** – 1 in., 5 rnds – 1 in. in stockinette st

Number of Complete Washer Cycles to Felt as Shown:
(Adjust as necessary to achieve desired size.) Less than 1. Agitate for about 9 minutes, then remove from washer and rinse in warm water.

Size before Felting:
13¼ in. to heel, 11¼ in. from heel to toe, 7 in. wide lying flat; Braided Hanger, approx 15 in. long

Size after Felting:
(NOTE: Sizes can vary due to individual washer cycles. Finished items that are too large can be felted again. Finished items that are too small can be stretched while wet to add about 15 percent additional length and/or width.) Stocking: 9½ in. to heel, 7¾ in. from heel to toe, 5 in. wide, lying flat; Braided Hanger: approx 12 in. long

Number of Yarn Strands Used:
1 throughout

NOTE: Carry the unused colors loosely on the inside of the work. Tie on new colors with 3-in. tails.

IT IS NECESSARY to work all solid-color rounds on the cuff, foot, heel, and toe with two strands, working every other stitch from separate balls of yarn (or from both ends of the same ball). Cast on the stitches, alternating every other ball (or from both ends of the same ball). The stocking will felt unevenly if all solid-color rounds are not stranded.

KNITTING INSTRUCTIONS

With Coal (alternating from 2 skeins, or working from both ends of 1 skein), and size 9 dpn, CO 76 sts, stranding every other st. Being careful not to twist the sts, divide the sts on 3 needles as evenly as possible, and join.

RND 1: K, stranding every other st.

Follow the chart, being sure to strand every solid-color row, until there are 5 peppermint-stick borders worked. Cut the yarns.

Heel

Dividing the Stitches for the Heel: Slip 16 sts from Needle #3 onto a new needle. Slip 16 sts from Needle #1 onto the same needle. These 32 sts will be the heel sts. Slip the remaining sts on Needle #2, or place them on a stitch holder, if desired.

HEEL FLAP ROW 1: Tie on Coal, stranding each st. Sl 1, K across. Turn.

HEEL FLAP ROW 2: Sl 1, P across. Turn.

Repeat Heel Flap Rows 1–2, 6 more times (14 rows total). End with a purl row.

HEEL TURNING ROW 1: Sl 1, K19, K2 tog, K1, turn.

HEEL TURNING ROW 2: Sl 1, P11, P2 tog, P1, turn.

HEEL TURNING ROW 3: Sl 1, K12, K2 tog, K1, turn.

Continue working the heel in this manner, working 1 more stitch before the decrease sequence on each row (either K2 tog, K1, turn, or P2 tog, P1, turn).

NOTE: It is not necessary to count the stitches before the decrease sequence if you understand that the K2 tog or P2 tog is **always** worked over the stitches before and after the gap. Continue until you have worked all the way across the needle. End with a purl row.

Gusset

NOTE: Work the Gusset rnds as follows: 2 rnds Coal, 1 rnd Coal/ Natural stranded (as per the chart), repeating those 3 rnds throughout the gusset decreases. End with 2 rnds Coal.

GUSSET RND 1: With Coal, sl 1, K across half of the sts. This needle will become Needle #3. Start a new needle and K the remaining heel sts. This needle is now Needle #1. Pick up and knit (stranding each st) 12 sts along the flap edge; K across Needle #2; with Needle #3, pick up and knit 12 sts (stranding each st) along the flap edge, K the remaining sts.

GUSSET RND 2: K to within 2 sts of the end of Needle #1, K2 tog, Work across Needle #2, K2 tog at the beginning of Needle #3, K to end.

GUSSET RND 3: K.

Repeat Gusset Rnds 2–3 until there are 16 sts left on Needles #1 and #3. Redistribute the sts. End established gusset pattern with 2 rnds of Coal.

Foot

Follow the chart for 2 Peppermint Stick Borders.

TOE DECREASE RND 1: Tie on Coal. Dec 4 sts evenly in the rnd. (72 sts remain)

TOE DECREASE RND 2 AND ALL EVEN TOE DECREASE RNDS: K.

TOE DECREASE RND 3: *K10, K2 tog*, repeat around. (66 sts remain)

TOE DECREASE RND 5: *K9, K2 tog*, repeat around. (60 sts remain)

TOE DECREASE RND 7: *K8, K2 tog*, repeat around. (54 sts remain)

TOE DECREASE RND 9: *K7, K2 tog*, repeat around. (48 sts remain)

Continue in this manner, working 1 less st before the decreases on all odd rnds, until there is just 1 st between the decreases and 12 sts remain. Cut a 12-in. tail. Thread the tail in a large-eye needle, and weave the remaining sts together. Tie off and weave the tail in on the inside of the stocking. Weave the topmost tails in. Trim the remaining tails to 1 in.

Braided Hanger

Cut 2 48-in. lengths each of Natural and Dove Heather. Cut 1 48-in. length each of Cranberry and Tomato. Fold each length in half, and divide as follows: 1 Natural and 1 Dove Heather, 1 Cranberry and 1 Tomato, 1 Natural and 1 Dove Heather. Tie all of the folded ends together, and braid the strands. Tie the strands together at the end.

FELTING

Place the stocking and the braided hanger in a mesh zippered lingerie bag and wash on the hot/cold cycle. Check the progress frequently and remove the pieces when the desired amount of felting has taken place. Remove from lingerie bag, rinse in warm water, and flatten and shape the stocking. Straighten the braided hanger. Allow the pieces to dry.

ASSEMBLY

Trim the felted, knotted ends from the braid. Fold the braid into a loop and hand-sew it to the upper edge of the stocking with matching thread. (NOTE: You can color the white thread with a permanent marker on the inside of the stocking to cover the stitching.) Tie a knot in each of the braided ends.

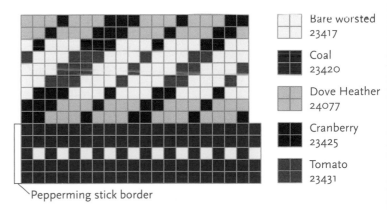

Peppermint stick border

	Bare worsted 23417
	Coal 23420
	Dove Heather 24077
	Cranberry 23425
	Tomato 23431

PEPPERMINT STICK CHRISTMAS STOCKING COLOR CHART

child-size gingham vest

Knit and felt the body of this child-size vest as a
tube, then cut the front opening, armholes, and neck shaping. Afterward, knit the ribbed bands separately and sew them in place. Finish with bright matching buttons for an adorable chill-chaser.

Yarn:
Knit Picks Wool of the Andes, 100% Peruvian wool, 50 g, 110 yd., 2 skeins each of #23437 Cherry Blossom, #23419 Hollyberry, #23766 Avocado, #23433 Fern, #24068 Cerulean, and #23434 Stream Knit Picks Bare—Peruvian Wool Worsted Weight, 100% Peruvian wool, 100 g, 220 yd., #23417 Natural, 2 skeins

Yarn Weight:
Worsted

Needles:
Size 11 (U.S.) circular, 24 in.
Size 7 (U.S.) straight, 14 in. (or circular)

Tools:
Stitch marker
Large-eye blunt needle
Sewing needle

Notions:
8 (9)½-in. buttons
Matching thread

Sizes:
Child 4–6 (approx 26-in. chest), 8–10 (approx 30-in. chest)

Unfelted Gauge:
Approx 3.5 sts = 1 in., approx 3.5 rows = 1 in. in stockinette st

Number of Complete Washer Cycles to Felt as Shown:
(Adjust as necessary to achieve desired size.) 1

Sizes before Felting:
21½ in. (25½ in.) long; 22¼ in. (26¼ in.) wide, with the knitted tube lying flat

Sizes after Felting:
(NOTE: Sizes can vary due to individual washer cycles. Finished items that are too large can be felted again. Finished items that are too small can be stretched while wet, to add about 15 percent additional length and/or width.)

14 in. (16 in.) long, 23½ in. (27½ in.) wide, cut open

Finished Vest Measurements:
Chest: 26 in. (30 in.); Back Length from Shoulder: 16½ in. (18½ in.); Armhole Length (measured from band outer edge): 7 in. (7½ in.)

Number of Yarn Strands Used:
1 throughout

NOTE: Strand the yarn **loosely** across the back of the work. Each rnd must have Fair Isle stranded stitching (including the CO and BO rnds) for the piece to felt uniformly. Do not strand the yarn vertically; instead, cut and tie new colors at the beginning of each new color section. Leave a 3-in. tail when you tie on new colors, and do not weave the loose ends in.

KNITTING INSTRUCTIONS

With size 11 circular needle and Cherry Blossom and Hollyberry, CO 160 (192) sts, following the chart (CO 4 sts Cherry Blossom, 4 sts Hollyberry throughout). Make sure the sts aren't twisted, place a stitch marker, and join. The beginning of the rnd will be the center front of the vest.

Work the vest body as per the chart until the piece measures 21½ in. (25½ in.) long.

BO in pattern (stranding the colors as you BO).

FELTING

Place the vest body in a large mesh zippered lingerie bag and wash on the hot/cold cycle. Check the progress frequently and remove when the desired amount of felting has taken place. Remove the vest body from the lingerie bag and cut the tube open along the center front line. The knitted-in design will look skewed and crooked right out of the washer. Don't worry—just pull and stretch and block the piece until the lines and edges are all straight. If some sections of the felted fabric pucker and can't be manually pulled into shape, you can carefully cut the felted floats on the back and pull and stretch the fabric again. Allow the body to dry. Trim any felted yarn ends flush with the fabric.

VEST BODY CUTTING AND SHAPING

1. Trim all edges straight and even.
2. Following the Gingham Vest Cutting chart, measure 4½ in. (5½ in.) in from one outer edge and mark at the upper edge. Measure 8 in. (8½ in.) down from that mark and cut for armhole. Measure 2 in. over from the lowest point of the armhole cut, and cut across. Measure 2 in. from the upper cut edge and mark. Cut from the upper edge mark to the lower cut. Repeat with the other armhole.

3. Measure 3 in. (4 in.) from the back armhole edge on both sides and mark. Find the center of the back neck edge and measure down 1 in. and mark. Cut a gently sloping neckline from the shoulder markings, so that the neckline is 1 in. deep at the center and 5 in. wide.

4. Measure 3 in. (4 in.) from the front armhole edge and mark. Measure 2 in. down along the front. Cut the front neckline in a slope from that mark, down 2 in. Repeat with the other side.

5. Fold vest in half vertically and check the armholes and neckline cuts. Trim to match if necessary.

BAND KNITTING INSTRUCTIONS

NOTE: The felted fabric will be too dense to pick up and knit the band stitches directly from the fabric. The bands are knitted separately and then sewn in place.

Armhole Bands (make 2)

With Natural and size 7 needles, CO 100 (110) sts. Work in K1, P1 ribbing for 7 rows. BO loosely. Weave in loose ends.

Neckband

With Natural and size 7 needles, CO 84 sts. Work as for Armhole Bands.

Bottom Band

With Natural and size 7 needles, CO 130 (150) sts. Work as for Armhole Bands, until Bottom Band measures 2½ in., or so that the total length of the Bottom Band and the felted vest body measure 16½ in. (18½ in.). BO loosely, weave in loose ends.

Left Front Band

With Natural and size 7 needles, CO 90 (102) sts. Work as for Armhole Bands for 14 rows. BO loosely, weave in loose ends.

Right Front Band (Buttonhole Band)

With Natural and size 7 needles, CO 90 (102) sts. Work as for Armhole Bands for 7 rows.

BUTTONHOLE ROW 1: Work 2 sts in patt, *YO, P2 tog, work 10 sts in patt*, repeat 6 (7) times, end with YO, P2 tog, work last 2 sts in patt.

BUTTONHOLE ROW 2: Work in patt, working each YO as a stitch.

Work even in ribbing until band is 14 rows. BO loosely, weave in loose ends.

ASSEMBLY

1. Evenly stretch Armhole Band around arm opening, with the **BO edge next to the felted fabric.** Pin in place and stitch along the outside with matching sewing thread. Whipstitch the inner edge to the band on the inside. Repeat with other Armhole Band.

2. Hold the front and back shoulder edge together, and hand-stitch the seam with sewing thread. Whipstitch the inside edges of the seam.

3. Evenly stretch the Neckband around the neck opening. Pin in place and stitch as for the Armhole Bands, with the **BO edge next to the felted fabric.**

4. Evenly stretch the Bottom Band around the bottom of the vest. Pin in place and stitch as for the Armhole Bands.

5. Evenly stretch the Left Front Band to the left front opening with the **CO edge next to the felted fabric edge.** Stitch as for the Armhole Bands.

6. Evenly stretch the Right Front (Buttonhole) Band to the right front opening with the **CO edge next to the felted fabric edge.** Stitch as for the Armhole Bands.

7. Sew the buttons in place

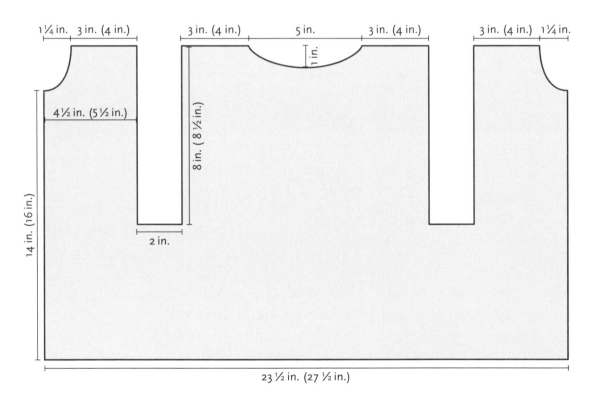

GINGHAM VEST CUTTING CHART

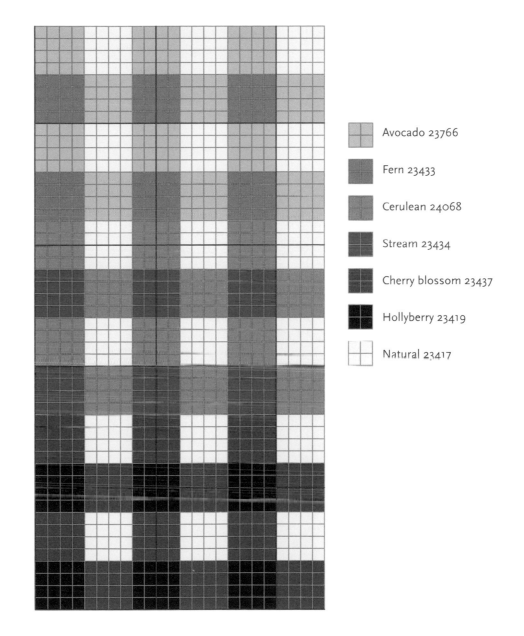

Avocado 23766

Fern 23433

Cerulean 24068

Stream 23434

Cherry blossom 23437

Hollyberry 23419

Natural 23417

GINGHAM VEST COLOR CHART

EXPLORING
embellishments

NOW IT'S TIME TO PLAY.
Take your finished knitted felt pieces and
DRESS THEM UP
with embroidery, beads, appliqué & needlefelting.
Turn a plain hat & bag

into a sweet **Frosting Hearts** set. Add beads and sequins to **Beaded Tiaras** and **Magic Wands** for your favorite little girl. Please that teen with funky **Needlefelted Fingerless Mittens** or adorable **appliquéd mittens and wristband.** Stay cozy in the **Berries and Vines Slippers** indoors, and outdoors with the **Beads and Scallops Hat.** Delight yourself with a lovely needlefelted **Cosmos Bag,** and decorate for the holidays with **Needlefelted Folk Art Santa Ornaments.** ● But as you make these items, think of the directions as guidelines only: Let your imagination run wild!

frosting hearts
hat & bag

What little girl wouldn't be enchanted with this

matching folk art earflap hat and bag? The hat and bag bodies are knitted and felted separately from the red garter-stitch hearts, then assembled after drying. After felting, dress this adorable combo up with chain stitching and beads.

Yarn:

Cascade 220, 100% Peruvian highland wool, 100 g, 220 yd., #8505 (white), 1 skein

Cascade 220 Quatro, 100% Peruvian highland wool, 100 g, 220 yd., #5013 (red), 1 skein

Small amount of off-white fingering-weight yarn (for chain-stitch embroidery)

Yarn Weight:

Worsted

Needles:

Size 9 (U.S.) dpn, 10 in.

Tools:

Large-eye blunt needle

Large-eye sharp needle

Beading needle

Needle threader (if desired, for beading needle)

Notions:

Sewing thread

1¾-In. Clover Magnet Tote Bag Closure

Cartwright's Sequins 4-mm flat square pink paillettes

Cartwright's Sequins iridescent off-white rocaille beads

Sizes:

One size fits most children ages 2 to 7

Unfelted Gauge:

Approx 4 sts = 1 in., 5.5 rnds = 1 in. in stockinette st

Number of Complete Washer Cycles to Felt as Shown:

(Adjust as necessary to achieve desired size.) 1

Sizes before Felting:

Hat: 9½ in. wide, 10 in. tall; Bag: 6¾ in. wide, 9¾ in. long; Earflap Hearts: 6 in. wide, 5 in. tall; Large Appliqué Hearts: 4½ in. wide, 4 in. tall; Medium Appliqué Heart: 3¾ in. wide, 3¼ in. tall; Small Appliqué Hearts: 3½ in. wide, 2¾ in. tall; Hat I-cords: 15 in. long, Bag I-cord; 20 in. long

Sizes after Felting:
(NOTE: Sizes can vary due to individual washer cycles. Finished items that are too large can be felted again. Finished items that are too small can be stretched while wet to add about 15 percent additional length and/or width.) Hat: 9 in. wide (lying flat), 7¼ in. tall; Bag: 6 in. wide (lying flat), 7 in. long; Earflap Hearts: 5¼ in. wide, 3½ in. tall; Large Appliqué Hearts: 3¾ in. wide, 2¾ in. tall; Medium Appliqué Heart: 3½ in. wide, 2½ in. tall; Small Appliqué Hearts: 3 in. wide, 2¼ in. tall; Hat I-cords: 12 in. long; Bag I-cord: 17 in. long

Number of Yarn Strands Used: 1 throughout

KNITTING INSTRUCTIONS

Hat

With size 9 dpn, and white, CO 80 sts. Divide as evenly as possible on 3 needles. Being careful not to twist the stitches, join.

RND 1: K.

Work even until hat measures 7 in.

DECREASE RND 1: *K6, K2 tog*, repeat around.
(70 sts remain)

DECREASE RNDS 2–3: K.

DECREASE RND 4: *K5, K2 tog*, repeat around.
(60 sts remain)

DECREASE RNDS 5–6: K.

DECREASE RND 7: *K4, K2 tog*, repeat around.
(50 sts remain)

DECREASE RNDS 8–9: K.

DECREASE RND 10: *K3, K2 tog*, repeat around.
(40 sts remain)

DECREASE RNDS 11–12: K.

DECREASE RND 13: *K2, K2 tog*, repeat around.
(30 sts remain)

DECREASE RNDS 14–15: K.

DECREASE RND 16: *K1, K2 tog*, repeat around.
(20 sts remain)

DECREASE RNDS 17–18: K.

DECREASE RND 19: *K2 tog*, repeat around.
(10 sts remain)

Cut a 12-in. tail. Thread the tail in a large-eye blunt needle, and weave the remaining stitches closed. Tighten and tie off on the inside of the hat.

Bag

With size 9 dpn and white, CO 60 sts. Divide on 3 needles. Being careful not to twist the stitches, join.

RND 1: K.

Work even until bag measures 6 in.

DECREASE RND 1: *K8, K2 tog*, repeat around.
(54 sts remain)

DECREASE RNDS 2–3: K.
DECREASE RND 4: *K7, K2 tog*, repeat around.
(48 sts remain)
DECREASE RNDS 5–6: K.
DECREASE RND 7: *K6, K2 tog*, repeat around.
(42 sts remain)
DECREASE RNDS 8–9: K.
DECREASE RND 10: *K5, K2 tog*, repeat around.
(36 sts remain)
DECREASE RNDS 11–12: K.
DECREASE RND 13: *K4, K2 tog*, repeat around.
(30 sts remain)
DECREASE RNDS 14–15: K.
DECREASE RND 16: *K3, K2 tog*, repeat around.
(24 sts remain)
DECREASE RNDS 17–18: K.
DECREASE RND 19: *K2, K2 tog*, repeat around.
(18 sts remain)
DECREASE RNDS 20–21: K.
DECREASE RND 22: *K1, K2 tog*, repeat around.
(12 sts remain)
DECREASE RNDS 23–24: K.
DECREASE RND 25: *K2 tog*, repeat around.
(6 sts remain)
Cut a 12-in. tail. Thread the tail in a large-eye blunt
needle, and weave the remaining stitches closed.
Tighten and tie off. Weave loose ends in on the inside of
the hat.

Earflap Heart (make 2)
With size 9 dpn and red, CO 25 sts.

ROW 1: K. Turn.
ROWS 2–14: Work even in garter st. (K every row)
DECREASE ROW 1: K2 tog, K to within last 2 sts on
the needle, K2 tog. Turn.
DECREASE ROW 2: K.
Repeat Decrease Rows 1–2 until 3 sts remain.
I-CORD ROW 1: Without turning the needle, slide the
sts to the right needle point, bring the yarn around the
back and to the beginning of the row, tighten. K across.
Do not turn.
Repeat I-Cord Row 1 until I-cord is 15 in. long.
LAST I-CORD ROW: Sl 1, K2 tog, PSSO.
Cut a 6-in. tail. Thread the tail in a large-eye blunt
needle, and weave through the remaining stitch. Tighten
and tie off. Thread tail inside the I-cord.

Large Appliqué Hearts (make 2)
With size 9 dpn and red, CO 19 sts.
ROW 1: K. Turn.
ROWS 2–12: Work even in garter st.
Decrease as for Earflap Heart until 3 sts rem.
LAST ROW: Sl 1, K2 tog, PSSO.
Cut a 6-in. tail. Thread the tail in a large-eye blunt
needle, and weave through the remaining stitch. Tighten
and tie off. Weave loose ends in on the wrong side of
the heart.

Medium Appliqué Heart (make 1)
With size 9 dpn and red, CO 17 sts.
ROW 1: K. Turn.
ROWS 2–10: Work even in garter st.
Decrease and finish as for Large Appliqué Hearts.

Small Appliqué Hearts (make 2)

With size 9 dpn and red, CO 15 sts.

ROW 1: K. Turn.

ROWS 2–8: Work even in garter st.

Decrease and finish as for Large Appliqué Hearts.

Bag Handle (make 1)

With size 9 dpn and red, CO 3 sts.

ROW 1: K.

ROW 2: Inc 1 st at the beginning and end of the row, K across.

ROW 3: K.

Continue increasing 1 st at either side of every other row until there are 17 sts.

Work even for 12 rows.

NEXT ROW: BO 7 sts, K3, BO 7 sts. Cut yarn.

I-CORD: Tie yarn at beginning of row.

Work I-cord for 20 in., as for Earflap Hearts.

NEXT ROW: Do not turn. Bring yarn around from back to beginning of row. CO 7 sts. K across those 7 sts, K3, CO 7 sts. Turn.

Work remainder of heart as for Medium Appliqué Heart.

FELTING

Place the hat and bag only in a mesh zippered lingerie bag and wash on the hot/cold cycle. Check the progress frequently and remove the hat and bag when the desired amount of felting has taken place. Hand-shape the hat and bag. Allow them to dry.

Felt the hearts, earflaps, and bag handle in a separate cycle from the hat and bag bodies to prevent color bleeding. Smooth and stretch the I-cords to straighten, if necessary. Lay the hearts flat on a smooth surface, pull and stretch the upper edges of each heart into a heart shape, and allow them to dry.

EMBROIDERY

Using off-white fingering-weight yarn threaded in a large-eye sharp needle, embroider a chain-stitch border $\frac{1}{4}$ in. to $\frac{1}{2}$ in. inside the outer edge of each heart. You may use a pencil to lightly draw in the curlicue shapes if you desire. Work only on the uppermost layer of the felted hearts; do not allow the white stitching to show on the wrong side of the hearts.

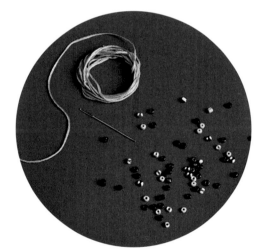

BEADING

Using white thread in a beading needle, sew random rocaille bead/paillette combos on each heart, inside the chain-stitch embroidery. Sew each bead as follows:

Bring the needle up from the back to the right side of the heart, thread through the center hole of the paillette, thread through a rocaille bead, bring the needle back through the center hole of the paillette, and tighten. Tie a small knot, and repeat until the center of each heart is filled with bead/paillette combos. Do not allow the white thread to show on the wrong side of the hearts. Sew several bead/paillette combos at the ends of the earflap I-cords.

HAT ASSEMBLY

Position the beaded/embroidered earflap hearts on either side of the hat lower edge, with about half of each heart hanging below the hat. Stitch firmly in place. Arrange 2 large and 2 small appliqué hearts on the hat, and stitch firmly in place.

BAG ASSEMBLY

According to the manufacturer's instructions, position and attach the magnetic closure pieces centered and ½ in. down from the upper edge of the bag opening. Position the beaded/embroidered handle over the closures on the front and back with about 3/4 in. of the heart extending above the bag opening. Stitch firmly in place. Position and stitch 1 medium appliqué heart on the front of the bag.

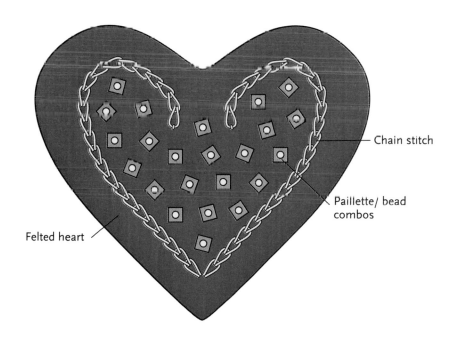

Chain stitch

Paillette/ bead combos

Felted heart

FELTED HEART EMBELLISHMENT GUIDE

field of flowers
mittens

You can adapt these mittens for all sizes by *varying the felting time. Lightly felted, they will fit adults; run them through another cycle, and they'll fit older children (but not toddlers). The asymmetrical felted appliqués turn these mittens into a field of flowers set against a blue sky. Wear them alone or over a pair of lightweight gloves for extra warmth.*

Yarn:
Knit Picks Merino Style, 100% Merino wool, 50 g, 123 yd., 1 skein each of #23452 Tide Pool, #23457 Pine, #23445 Mint, #23454 Iris, #23446 Cornflower, and #23449 Petal

Yarn Weight:
DK

Needles:
Size 8 (U.S.) dpn
Size 8 (U.S.) straight

Tools:
1 stitch marker
Small stitch holder (or large safety pin)

Large-eye blunt needle
Sewing needle

Notions:
Matching sewing thread
Mainstay Crafts glass E beads, #80224-07 Black

Sizes: Youth to Adult

Unfelted Gauge:
Approx 4.5 sts = 1 in., 6 rows = 1 in. in stockinette st

Number of Complete Washer Cycles to Felt as Shown:
(Adjust as necessary to achieve desired size.) Less than 1 for Adult size (remove after 7 minutes of

agitation). Check frequently for smaller sizes, remove when desired amount of felting has occurred (may take more than 1 full cycle to felt to proper child size). Swatches and I-cord: 1

Sizes before Felting:
Mitten: 11¾ in. long, 4¾ in. wide (lying flat); Swatches: 6¼ in. wide, 4¾ in. long; I-cord: 49 in. long

Sizes after Felting:
(NOTE: Sizes can vary due to individual washer cycles. Finished items that are too large can be

felt again. Finished items that are too small can be stretched while wet to add about 15 percent additional length and/or width.)

Adult: approx 9½ in. long, 4¼ in. wide; Swatches: 5 in. wide, 3½ in. long; I-cord: 48 in. long. Children's sizes depend on the amount of felting.

Number of Yarn Strands Used: 1 throughout

KNITTING INSTRUCTIONS

Mitten (make 2)

With size 8 dpn and Mint, CO 48 sts. Divide evenly on dpn without twisting the sts, join.

Work 30 rnds in stockinette st.

THUMB GUSSET ROW 1: Pick up and knit 1, inc 1, place marker, K around. (2 sts increased)

THUMB GUSSET ROW 2 AND ALL EVEN GUSSET ROWS: K.

THUMB GUSSET ROW 3: Pick up and knit 1, K to the marker, pick up and knit 1, move marker, K around. (2 sts increased)

Continue Thumb Gusset Rows 2–3 until there are 13 sts before the marker.

NEXT RND: K.

NEXT RND: Tie off Mint. Tie on Tide Pool. K.

Work 3 more rnds even.

HAND RND 1: Place the 13 thumb sts on a small stitch holder. CO 1, K around.

Work even for 28 rnds.

DECREASE RND 1: *K6, K2 tog*, repeat around. (42 sts remain)

DECREASE RND 2 AND ALL EVEN DECREASE RNDS UNTIL OTHERWISE NOTED: K.

DECREASE RND 3: *K5, K2 tog*, repeat around. (36 sts remain)

DECREASE RND 5: *K4, K2 tog*, repeat around. (30 sts remain)

DECREASE RND 7: *K3, K2 tog*, repeat around. (24 sts remain)

DECREASE RND 9: *K2, K2 tog*, repeat around. (18 sts remain)

DECREASE RND 10: *K1, K2 tog*, repeat around. (12 sts remain)

Cut a 12-in. tail. Thread the tail in a large-eye needle and weave through the remaining sts. Tighten and tie off on the inside of the mitten. Tighten the knots at the color change, and trim. Trim the tails, but do not weave them in.

THUMB: Place the 13 sts on size 8 dpn. With Tide Pool, pick up and knit 3 sts in the gap. Divide the sts as evenly as possible. (16 sts)

Work even for 10 rnds.

THUMB DECREASE RND 1: *K2 tog*, repeat around. (8 sts remain)

THUMB DECREASE RND 2: *K2 tog*, repeat around. (4 sts remain)

Tighten and tie off as for the mitten.

SWATCHES

Make 1 each of Petal, Iris, and Cornflower.
With size 8 straight needles, CO 30 sts. Work even in stockinette st for 30 rows. BO. Trim yarn ends.

I-Cord

With size 8 dpn and Pine, CO 3.
ROW 1: K across.
ROW 2: Slide the sts to the right side of the needle, bring the yarn from the back of the sts and tighten, K across. Repeat Row 2 until the I-cord is 49 in. long.
LAST ROW: Sl 1, K2 tog, PSSO. Cut tail, weave through the remaining loop, and tighten. Weave the ends back inside the I-cord.

FELTING

Place items in a mesh zippered lingerie bag and wash on the hot/cold cycle. Check the progress frequently and remove the mittens when the desired amount of felting has taken place (7 minutes of agitation for the Adult size; allow the felting to continue for smaller mittens, possibly even another whole washer cycle for Child sizes). Let the swatches and I-cord felt for an entire washer cycle. Rinse the items removed earlier with warm water. Pull the pieces into shape, making upper and lower swatch edges straight. Trim the felted yarn ends. Allow items to dry.

FINISHING

1. Trace 4 Flower shapes on the back of the Iris and Cornflower felted swatches. Cut them out. Trace 8 Center shapes on the back of the Petal felted swatch. Cut them out.

2. With matching sewing thread, stitch one Petal center to each flower. With matching sewing thread, sew 3 black beads to the middle of each flower center.

3. Following the photo on p. 126, cut and pin the felted Pine I-cord in place for flower stems on the backs of the mittens. *NOTE: Vary the curves and placement of the stems so that the mittens do not match exactly.*

4. With matching sewing thread, stitch the Pine I-cord stems in place.

5. With matching sewing thread, stitch the flowers in place on the I-cord stems.

VARY THE CURVES and placement of the I-cord stems so that the mittens do not match exactly.

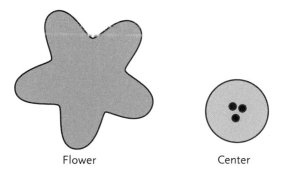

Flower   Center

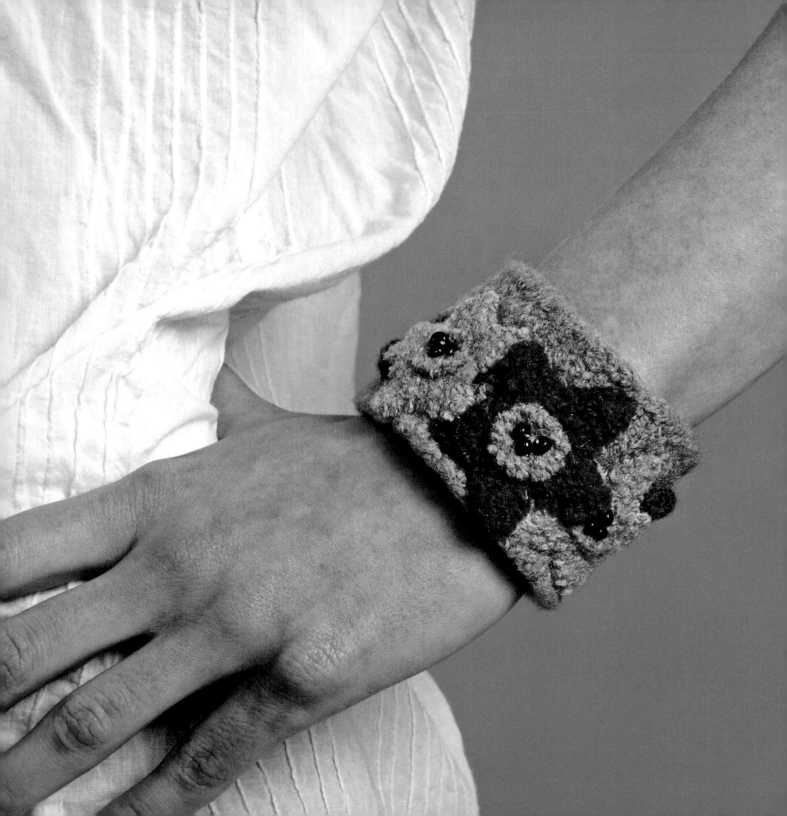

field of flowers
wristband

Use yarn and felted scraps left over
from other items or swatches to make this adorable wristband. We used materials from the Field of Flowers Mittens, but you can use any yarn and felted scraps for this quickie project.

Yarn:
See Field of Flowers Mittens (p.127) for yarn requirements, or use any feltable DK-weight yarn.

Yarn Weight:
DK

Needles:
Size 8 (U.S.) straight

Tools:
Large-eye blunt needle
Sewing needle

Notions:
Matching sewing thread

Mainstay Crafts glass E beads, #80224-07 Black
2 in. of ½-in.-wide Velcro® fastener

Sizes:
One size fits all

Unfelted Gauge:
Approx 4.5 sts = 1 in., 6 rows = 1 in. in stockinette st

Number of Complete Washer Cycles to Felt as Shown: 1

Sizes before Felting:
Approx 10 in. wide, 3 in. long

Sizes after Felting:
(NOTE: Sizes can vary due to individual washer cycles. Finished items that are too large can be felted again. Finished items that are too small can be stretched while wet to add about 15 percent additional length and/or width.)
Approx 9¾ in. wide, 2 in. long (trim length after felting)

Number of Yarn Strands Used:
1 throughout

KNITTING INSTRUCTIONS

With any color DK yarn (Knit Picks Merino Style Cornflower is used here) and size 8 needles, CO 50 sts. Work in stockinette st for 8 rows.
Tie off Cornflower, tie on Pine (or any color DK yarn). Work even for 2 rows.
Tie off Pine, tie on Cornflower. Work even for 8 rows. BO. Trim the yarn ends but do not weave them in.

SWATCHES

Use leftover pieces from other projects or knit more, as for the Field of Flowers Mittens.

I-Cord

Use leftover pieces from other projects, or knit 12 in., as for the Field of Flowers Mittens.

FELTING

Place items in a mesh zippered lingerie bag and wash on the hot/cold cycle. Check the progress frequently and remove the wristband when the desired amount of felting has taken place. Flatten the wristband, making the upper and lower edges straight. Trim the felted yarn ends. Allow the wristband to dry.

FINISHING

1. Measure the wristband and trim the ends so that it fits comfortably with about a ½-in. overlap.
2. Trace 2 Flowers (from the Field of Flowers Mitten pattern) on the back of the leftover Petal swatch. Trace 1 Flower on the back of the leftover Iris swatch. Cut them out. Trace 3 Center shapes on the back of the leftover Iris swatch. Cut them out.
3. With matching sewing thread, stitch one Iris center to each flower. With matching sewing thread, stitch 3 black beads to the middle of each flower center.
4. Following the Wristband Appliqué Chart, cut and pin the felted Pine I-cord in place for the leaves.
5. With matching sewing thread, stitch the Pine I-cord leaves in place.
6. With matching sewing thread, stitch the flowers in place on the I-cord stems.
7. Sew the Velcro fastener in the back overlap.

FIELD OF FLOWERS WRISTBAND APPLIQUÉ GUIDE

beaded tiaras &
magic wands

Expand your little princess's magical
wardrobe with these whimsical beaded tiaras and magic wands.

Yarn:

Pink Set: Cascade 220 Quatro, 100% Peruvian highland wool, 100 g, 220 yd., #5012 (pink), 1 skein

Blue Set: Cascade 220 Quatro, 100% Peruvian highland wool, 100 g, 220 yd., #5018 (blue), 1 skein

Carry-along metallic filament (any brand)

Yarn Weight:

Worsted

Needles:

Size 11 (U.S.) straight

Tools:

Large-eye blunt needle
Large-eye sharp needle

Beading needle and threader (if desired)

Notions for Each Set:

Matching sewing thread ½-in.-wide matching ribbon, 2 yd.
Small amount of polyester fiberfill
1½ in. of 1-in.-wide Velcro fastener
Small paintbrush
One 12-in.-long, ¼-in.-diameter wooden dowel
Craft glue

Notions for Blue Set:

DecoArt™ Crafter's Acrylic™ paint, #DCA43 Dark Turquoise
Cartwright's Sequins 15-mm blue almond beads
Cartwright's Sequins silver glass rocaille beads

Mainstay Crafts glass E beads, 30 g tube, #80224-42 Blue/Green

Notions for Pink Set:

DecoArt Crafter's Acrylic paint, #DCA67 Thistle Blossom
Cartwright's Sequins 5-mm silver hologram flower
Cartwright's Sequins iridescent fuchsia rocaille beads
Mainstay Crafts glass E beads, 30 g tube, #80224-47 Sweetheart

Finished Sizes:

Wands: approx 13 in. long; Star approx 5 in. wide
Blue Tiara: 19½ in. to 23 in. long, 2 in. high
Pink Tiara: 19½ in. to 23 in. long, 2¾ in. high

Unfelted Gauge:

Approx 3.5 sts = 1 in., 4 rows = 1 in. in stockinette st

Number of Complete Washer Cycles to Felt as Shown:

(Adjust as necessary to achieve desired size.) 1 for wands, 2 for tiaras

Sizes before Felting:

Wand squares: 8 in. wide, 9¼ in. long

Blue Tiara: Approx 39 in. long, points 3½ in. high

Pink Tiara: Approx 39 in. long, points 5 in. high

Sizes after Felting:

(NOTE: Sizes can vary due to individual washer cycles. Finished items that are too large can be felted again. Finished items that are too small can be stretched while wet to add about 15 percent additional length and/or width.)

Wand squares: 5¾ in. wide, 6½ in. long

Blue Tiara: 19 in. to 23 in., points 2 in. high

Pink Tiara: 19 in. to 23 in., points 2¾ in. high

Number of Yarn Strands Used:

1 strand yarn and 1 strand metallic filament held together throughout

KNITTING INSTRUCTIONS

Wand Squares (make 2 for each wand)

With desired color yarn and 1 strand of metallic filament, and size 11 needles, CO 30 sts. Work in stockinette st until piece measures 9 in. long. BO all sts. Trim yarn ends closely, but do not weave the ends in.

Blue Tiara

With blue yarn and 1 strand of metallic filament, and size 11 needles, CO 8 sts.

Work in stockinette st for 5½ in., ending with a WS row.

POINT INCREASE ROW 1 (RS): Inc 1 st, K across.

POINT INCREASE ROW 2 (WS): P.

Rep Point Increase Rows 1–2 until there are 13 sts.

Work 2 rows even in stockinette st.

POINT DECREASE ROW 1 (RS): K2 tog, K across.

POINT DECREASE ROW 2 (WS): P.

Rep Point Decrease Rows 1–2 until 8 sts remain.

Work 2 rows even in stockinette st.

Repeat entire Point Increase and Decrease sequence 3 times.

Work stockinette st for 5½ in.

BO. Trim the yarn ends closely, but do not weave the yarn ends in.

Pink Tiara

With pink yarn and 1 strand of metallic filament, and size 11 needles, CO 8 sts.

Work in stockinette st for 5½ in., ending with a WS row.

POINT INCREASE ROW 1 (RS): Inc 1 st, K across.

POINT INCREASE ROW 2 (WS): P.

Rep Point Increase Rows 1–2 until there are 18 sts.

Work 2 rows even in stockinette st.

POINT DECREASE ROW 1 (RS): K2 tog, K across.
POINT DECREASE ROW 2 (WS): P.

Rep Point Decrease Rows 1–2 until 8 sts remain.

Work 2 rows even in stockinette st.

Repeat entire Point Increase and Decrease sequence 2 times.

Finish as for the Blue Tiara.

FELTING

Place all items in a small mesh zippered lingerie bag and wash on the hot/cold cycle. Check the progress frequently and remove items when the desired amount of felting has taken place. Items may need one or more completed washer cycles to reach desired size. Remove pieces from lingerie bag and pull them into shape, making edges straight and points even. Trim any felted yarn ends flush with the fabric. Allow all pieces to dry.

WAND BEADING

Blue Wand

Cut 2 stars from the felted Wand Squares, according to the pattern. Sew the beads on the right side of one cut star as per the Blue Wand Beading Guide, using matching thread and a beading needle. To sew the almond shapes, bring the needle up from the wrong side of the fabric, through one hole in the almond. Thread the needle through a silver rocaille bead, then back through the same hole in the almond, and tighten. Repeat with the other hole. Knot the thread every few beads for security.

Pink Wand

Cut and bead as for the Blue Wand, following the Pink Wand Beading Guide. To sew the silver hologram flowers, bring the needle up from the wrong side of the fabric through the center hole of the flower. Thread the needle through a light fuchsia rocaille bead, then back through the center hole, and tighten. Alternate clear and

FULLY FELTED FABRIC has no grain. If you are cutting appliqué pieces from solid-color felted swatches or scraps, the patterns can be placed any direction on the fabric.

white glass E beads as shown on the diagram. Alternate pink and red glass E beads as shown on the diagram.

WAND ASSEMBLY

1. Using the proper color paint, paint the 12-in. wooden dowel. Allow the paint to dry. Brush on another coat if desired. Sand lightly if needed.
2. With matching thread, stitch over the dowel, positioned up the center and on the wrong side of the unbeaded star. Dot the thread and dowel with glue. Allow to dry.
3. With matching thread, hand-stitch the front and back of the star together (right sides out) around the outside edge. Leave a 2-in. opening. Stuff lightly but evenly with polyester fiberfill. Stitch the opening closed.
4. Draw a line of glue around the painted dowel at the bottom edge of the star. Wrap matching ribbon around the dowel at that point. Draw a thin line of glue down the back length of the dowel. Wrap the ribbon around the length of the dowel, smoothing the ribbon into the glue as you wind. At the bottom, draw another thin line of glue around the lower edge and smooth the ribbon in place, trimming to fit. You can hold the bottom of the ribbon in place with a rubber band as it dries.
5. Cut the remaining ribbon into 2 equal lengths. Hold the lengths together and tie them, with the knot in the center front, just under the star. Trim the ribbon ends in a point. Dot the ribbon knot with glue to hold in place.

TIARA BEADING

Refer to the photo on page 134 for the tiara design and color, sew beads as shown.

TIARA ASSEMBLY

Trim the extended edges of the tiara so that it measures at least 1 in. longer than the desired head circumference. Overlap the back edges of the tiara and sew Velcro in the opening.

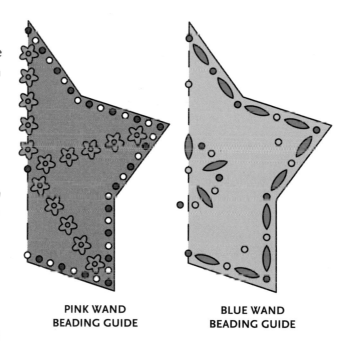

PINK WAND BEADING GUIDE   **BLUE WAND BEADING GUIDE**

(Enlarge each 30% if photocopying.)

beads & scallops hat

Knit this hat quickly with large needles.

The scalloped and beaded edge gives the hat a funky, retro feel.

Yarn:

Decadent Fibers Crème Puff, 20% mohair/79% Merino blend/1% nylon, 8 oz., 490 yd., Blueberry Buckle (purple and green variegated), 1 skein

Knit Picks Wool of the Andes Bulky Hand Dyed, 100% Peruvian wool, 100 g, 137 yd., #23952 Ireland (or any other green feltable wool yarn), a few yards

Yarn Weight:

Bulky

Needles:

Size 15 (U.S.) circular, 16 in., and/or size 15 (U.S.) dpn, 12 in.

Tools:

Large-eye blunt needle

Sewing needle

Beading needle

Notions:

Mainstay Crafts glass E bead mix, 28 g tube, #80244-02 Pink & Blue Matching thread

Sizes: Adult S (Adult L)

Unfelted Gauge:

2.5 sts = 1 in., 3 rnds = 1 in. in stockinette st

Number of Complete Washer Cycles to Felt as Shown:

(Adjust as necessary to achieve desired size.) Less than 1. Agitate 5–8 minutes, remove from washer, and rinse in lukewarm water.

Sizes before Felting:

Hat: 14 in. long, approx 11 in. wide, lying flat (14 in. long, approx 12 in. wide, lying flat); Petals: $3^3/4$ in. long, $2^1/2$ in. wide

Sizes after Felting:

(NOTE: Sizes can vary due to individual washer cycles. Finished items that are too large can be felted again. Finished items that are too small can be stretched while wet to add about 15 percent additional length and/or width.) Hat: 8 in. long with cuff folded up, $9^3/4$ in. wide, lying flat (8 in. long with cuff folded up, $10^3/4$ wide, lying flat); Petals: $2^3/4$ in. long, $1^3/4$ in. wide

Number of Yarn Strands Used:

1 for hat and petals, 2 for flower center

KNITTING INSTRUCTIONS

Hat

With Blueberry Buckle and size 15 needles, CO 54 (60) sts. Make sure the stitches are not twisted, divide evenly if using dpns, and join.

RND 1–5: K.

SCALLOP RND 6 (ALL SIZES): K6, bring yarn around the lower edge of the knitting and up through the center of the work, pull tightly and repeat around (the yarn will wrap around the piece and make a scallop).

K every rnd until piece measures 9½ in. (all sizes).

DECREASE RND 1: *K7 (8)*, K2 tog*, repeat around. (48, 54 sts remain)

DECREASE RND 2 AND ALL EVEN DECREASE RNDS: K.

DECREASE RND 3: *K6 (7), K2 tog*, repeat around. (42, 48 sts remain)

DECREASE RND 5: *K5 (6), K2 tog*, repeat around. (36, 42 sts remain)

DECREASE RND 7: *K4 (5), K2 tog*, repeat around. (30, 36 sts remain)

DECREASE RND 9: *K3 (4), K2 tog*, repeat around. (24, 30 sts remain)

DECREASE RND 11: *K2 (3), K2 tog*, repeat around. (18, 24 sts remain)

DECREASE RND 13: *K1 (2), K2 tog*, repeat around. (12, 18 sts remain)

NEXT RND (LARGE SIZE ONLY): *K1, K2 tog*, repeat around. (12 sts remain)

Cut a 12-in. tail and thread through a large-eye needle.

Weave the tail through the remaining sts, tighten, and tie off on the inside of the hat. Weave in the tail on the lower edge.

Petals (make 3)

With size 15 needles and Blueberry Buckle, CO 3.

ROW 1: K, turn.

ROW 2: P, turn.

ROW 3: K1, inc 1, K1, inc 1, K1, turn. (5 sts)

ROW 4: P, turn.

ROW 5: K1, inc 1, K3, inc 1, K 1, turn. (7 sts)

Work 4 rows even in stockinette st.

DECREASE ROW 1: K2 tog, K3, K2 tog, turn. (5 sts)

DECREASE ROW 2: P, turn.

DECREASE ROW 3: Sl 1, K2 tog, PSSO.

Cut a 6-in. tail, and thread through the remaining loop and tighten. Trim tails to 1 in.

Flower Center (make 1):

With size 15 needles and 2 strands of green held together, CO 3. Work 4 rows stockinette st. BO. Tie beginning and ending tails tightly together to make a ball. Trim the tail ends to 1 in.

FELTING

Place hat, petals, and flower center in a mesh zippered lingerie bag and wash on the hot/cold cycle. Check the progress frequently and remove the items when the desired amount of felting has taken place. Rinse in lukewarm water and spin to remove excess moisture. Pull the hat into shape, emphasizing the scallops on the edge. Fold the cuff up 1½ in. or desired amount. Smooth and flatten the petals. Shape the center into a flat circle. Allow items to dry. You can place the hat on a foam head form, or stuff it with plastic bags to hold the shape as it dries.

ASSEMBLY & FINISHING

1. With matching sewing thread, enhance the scallops if necessary by sewing over the edge and tightening the thread at each scallop indent.
2. Following the Beads and Scallops Hat Appliqué Beading Guide below, overlap the petals and tack together with sewing thread. Place the flower center as shown in the illustration and tack in place.
3. With sewing thread, tack the assembled petals and center to the side of the hat, just above the scalloped edge. Tack the petals down in several places, but leave the upper edges loose so that they curl just a bit.
4. With a beading needle, sew beads randomly in the flower center. With a beading needle, sew a line of 3 beads up the center of each petal as shown.
5. With a beading needle, sew 3 beads to each scallop indent as shown in the photo on p. 138.

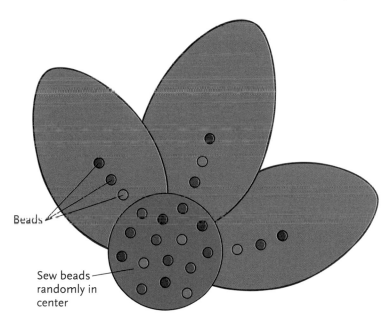

Beads

Sew beads randomly in center

BEADS AND SCALLOPS HAT APPLIQUÉ AND BEADING GUIDE

berries & vines
slippers

Knit and felt these simple slippers,

then dress them up with needlefelted berries and vines.

Yarn:
Cascade 220, 100% Peruvian highland wool, 100 g, 220 yd., #1208
(light brown), 2 (2, 3) skeins

Yarn Weight:
Worsted

Needles:
Size 11 (U.S.), dpn, 10 in.

Tools:
Large-eye blunt needle

Notions:
Medium-gauge needlefelting
needle
Two 4-in. by 4-in. by 6-in. foam
pieces Small amounts of olive
green and orange wool fleece

Small amounts of burgundy and
grass green wool yarn

Sizes:
Ladies S, shoe size 5–6 (M, shoe
size 7–8; L, shoe size 9–10)

Unfelted Gauge:
3.5 sts =1 in., 4 rnds = 1 in. in
stockinette st

**Number of Complete Washer
Cycles to Felt as Shown:**
(Adjust as necessary to achieve
desired size.) 2

Sizes before Felting:
13 in. (15 in., 17 in.) long, 6 in.
wide, lying flat (all sizes)

Sizes after Felting:
(NOTE: Sizes can vary due to
individual washer cycles. Finished
items that are too large can be
felted again. Finished items that
are too small can be stretched
while wet to add about 15 percent
additional length and/or width.)
8½ in. (9½ in., 10½ in.) long,
5 in. wide, lying flat (all sizes)

Number of Yarn Strands Used:
2 throughout

KNITTING INSTRUCTIONS

NOTE: The same number of sts are cast on for all sizes. Larger sizes have a longer foot.

With 2 strands of yarn held together, and size 11 needles, CO 38 sts. Divide as evenly as possible on 3 needles, make sure the stitches are not twisted, and join.

RND 1: K.

DIVIDE FOR HEEL: K 20 sts. Place the remaining sts on a single needle. Using the 20 sts for the heel, turn, and begin on the wrong side.

HEEL FLAP ROW 1: Sl 1, P across, turn.

HEEL FLAP ROW 2: Sl 1, K across, turn.

Work a total of 15 Heel Flap Rows, ending with a purl row, turn.

HEEL TURNING ROW 1: Sl 1, K11, K2 tog, K1, turn.

HEEL TURNING ROW 2: Sl 1, P5, P2 tog, P1, turn.

HEEL TURNING ROW 3: Sl 1, K6, K2 tog, K1, turn.

Continue in this way, working 1 more st before the decrease (either *K2 tog, K1, turn*, or *P2 tog, P1, turn*) on each row. Continue until you have worked across the entire set of heel sts. End with a purl row.

GUSSET RND 1: Sl 1, K half of the heel sts. These sts are now Needle #3. Start a new needle and K the remaining heel sts. Pick up and knit 9 sts along the heel flap. These sts are now Needle #1. K across Needle #2 (the sts held in reserve). Pick up and knit 9 sts along the heel flap, K the remaining sts on Needle #3.

GUSSET RND 2: K to within 2 sts of the end of Needle #1, K2 tog, K across Needle #2, on Needle #3, K2 tog, K to the end.

GUSSET RND 3 AND ALL ODD GUSSET RNDS: K. Rep Gusset Rnds 2–3 until there are 10 sts left on Needles #1 and #3. The stitch number on Needle #2 does not change. Redistribute the sts as evenly as possible on the 3 needles.

Work even until the slipper measures 7¼ in. (9¼ in., 11¼ in.) from the beginning of the gusset.

TOE DECREASE RND 1: Dec 2 sts evenly in rnd. (36 sts remain)

TOE DECREASE RND 2: *K4, K2 tog*, repeat around. (30 sts remain)

TOE DECREASE RND 3 AND ALL ODD TOE DECREASE RNDS: K.

TOE DECREASE RND 4: *K3, K2 tog*, repeat around. (24 sts remain)

TOE DECREASE RND 6: *K2, K2 tog*, repeat around. (18 sts remain)

TOE DECREASE RND 8: *K1, K2 tog*, repeat around. (12 sts remain)

Cut yarns, leaving a 12-in. tail. Thread tail yarns in a large-eye needle and weave through the remaining sts. Tighten and tie off on the inside of the slipper. Weave in the tails at the foot opening.

FELTING

Place slippers in a mesh zippered bag and wash on the hot/cold cycle. Remove them when the desired amount of felting has taken place. Pull slippers into shape. Try the wet slippers on. If the opening is too small, stretch it. You may stuff the slippers with plastic bags to hold the shape while drying. Allow them to dry.

NEEDLEFELTING INSTRUCTIONS

NOTE: If you do not have wool fleece, you may substitute wool yarn for the leaves and berries: Simply tack and fill in the areas with yarn.

1. Place 4-in. by 4-in. by 6-in. foam in the opening of each slipper. Following the Berries and Vines Needlefelting Guide on p. 146, tack burgundy wool yarn in a loose curlicue pattern around the foot opening with a medium-gauge needlefelting needle and an upright stabbing motion. The vines need not be symmetrical, and the slippers do not need to be mirror images of each other. If you don't like the design or placement of the curlicue, pull it out, reform the shape, and anchor it again. After the vine has been tacked in place, go back and anchor the yarn firmly by poking the yarn along the entire length of the design. This may take several hundred jabs. The vine is firmly embedded when the yarn is uniformly tight and even. If portions of the yarn still look loose and unformed, continue jabbing. If you "over-poke" the yarn and the line looks faint or disappears entirely, simply cut a small piece of yarn and needlefelt that over the original line.

2. Pull off a small amount of olive green wool fleece or roving and loosely twist it into a leaf shape. Place the leaf shape below the needlefelted vine and tack in place with the needlefelting needle. Once you have the leaf shape in place, go back and anchor the leaf firmly by poking over the entire surface of the leaf. You can shape and form the leaf as you needlefelt. Add more wool fleece if needed. Repeat with as many leaves as you want on your slippers (the slippers shown here have 5 leaves apiece).

3. Tack grass green wool yarn from the vine above each leaf, down the center of each leaf. Trim the grass green wool yarn, and anchor firmly with the needlefelting needle, as for the vine.

4. Pull off small amounts of orange wool fleece and roll loosely in a small ball for the berries. Tack each berry to the slipper, near the vines. You can group them singly, in pairs, or in trios. Anchor the berries firmly as for the leaves. You may add more fleece if desired.

5. With burgundy yarn, anchor and needlefelt stems from the vine to the center of each berry.

6. Carefully remove the foam from the slippers. Each needlefelted area will have to be detached from the foam by placing your fingers in between the slipper and the foam and gently pushing the embedded areas up.

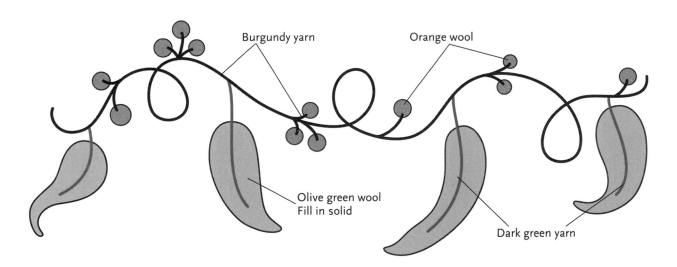

Burgundy yarn

Orange wool

Olive green wool
Fill in solid

Dark green yarn

BERRIES AND VINES NEEDLEFELTING GUIDE

needlefelted
fingerless mittens

Wear these funky needlefelted fingerless
mittens over gloves for extra warmth and color, or go naked as the weather permits.

Yarn:
Knit Picks Merino Style, 100% Merino wool, 50 g, 123 yd., #23465 Harvest, 2 skeins; #23460 Nutmeg (Brown) and #23453 Crocus, 1 skein each; #23456 Coal (or any black wool yarn), a few yards

Yarn Weight:
DK

Needles:
Size 8 (U.S.) dpn, 8 in.

Tools:
1 stitch marker
1 small stitch holder
Large-eye blunt needle

Notions:
8-in. by 10-in. piece of heavy foam, 4 in. thick
Fine-gauge needlefelting needle

Size:
One size fits all adults

Unfelted Gauge:
5 sts = 1 in., 6 rnds = 1 in. in stockinette st

Number of Complete Washer Cycles to Felt as Shown:
(Adjust as necessary to achieve desired size.) 2

Size before Felting:
11 in. long, 6 in. wide, lying flat

Size after Felting:
(NOTE: Sizes can vary due to individual washer cycles. Finished items that are too large can be felted again. Finished items that are too small can be stretched while wet to add about 15 percent additional length and/or width.)
7½ in. long, 4¼ in. wide, lying flat

Number of Yarn Strands Used:
1 throughout

STRIPE PATTERN

10 rnds Nutmeg, 10 rnds Harvest, 10 rnds Crocus, 10 rnds Harvest, 10 rnds Nutmeg, 10 rnds Harvest, 10 rnds Crocus, finish with Harvest

KNITTING INSTRUCTIONS

Mittens (make 2)

With Nutmeg, CO 60 sts. Divide evenly on needles, making sure that the stitches are not twisted, and join.

RND 1: K.

Work even in Stripe Pattern for 40 rnds total.

GUSSET RND 1: Inc 1, K1, inc 1, place marker (2 sts increased), K around.

GUSSET RND 2 AND ALL EVEN GUSSET RNDS: K.

GUSSET RND 3 AND ALL ODD GUSSET RNDS: Inc 1, K to marker, inc 1, move marker, K around. (2 sts increased)

Repeat Gusset Rnds 2–3 until there are 17 sts before the marker.

Work even 4 more rnds.

NEXT RND: Place the 17 thumb gusset sts on a small holder, CO 1 st, K around.

Work even 18 rnds. BO.

Thumb

Using the same color yarn as the gusset sts, place the 17 thumb gusset sts on needles, pick up and knit 3 sts in the gap between the thumb sts and the upper part of the hand. Divide the sts as evenly as possible on the needles.

Work even 6 rnds (do not change yarn colors).

BO. Weave in the BO and CO tails along the edges.

FELTING

Place mittens in a small mesh zippered lingerie bag and wash on the hot/cold cycle. Check the progress frequently and remove the mittens when the desired amount of felting has taken place. Pull the mittens into shape, making upper and lower edges straight. Trim any remaining yarn ends inside the mittens. Allow the mittens to dry.

NEEDLEFELTING INSTRUCTIONS

NOTE: The needlefelting illustration is a guideline only. The embellishments are freeform, and the mittens need not be mirror images of each other.

NOTE: Needlefelting needles are barbed and very sharp. Use caution when needlefelting.

1. Cut two 3½-in. by 8-in. strips from the foam block. Fit one mitten over each cut piece (the fit will be snug). Cut smaller pieces from the remaining foam and stuff the thumbs and gussets firmly with foam.

2. Follow the Fingerless Mittens Needlefelting Guide on p. 150, or make up designs as you go. Cut an 8-in. piece of black yarn and form a curlicue on the back of one mitten. Using a fine-gauge needle, poke through the yarn and mitten and into the foam with an upright stabbing motion. Repeat every ⅛ in. along the yarn curlicue to anchor the yarn in place. If you want your mitten designs to match, repeat with the other mitten (making sure to mirror-image your curlicue). If you

don't like the design or placement of the curlicue, pull it out, reform the shape, and anchor it again.

3. Once you are happy with the shape of the curlicue, poke the yarn repeatedly along the entire length of the curlicue. The yarn is anchored fully when the yarn is uniformly tight and even. It will take several hundred jabs of the needle to fully needlefelt the curlicue. If portions of the yarn still look loose and unformed, continue jabbing.

4. Repeat with the other curlicues until you are happy with the design. If you "over-poke" the yarn and the line looks faint or disappears entirely, simply cut a small piece of yarn and needlefelt that over the original line.

5. Carefully loosen the mitten from the foam, and remove the foam.

6. Repeat on the back of the other mitten. Remember that the mittens need not be mirror images of each other.

FINGERLESS MITTENS NEEDLEFELTING GUIDE

cosmos bag

Needlefelted spirals float like galaxies

in the night sky on this great handbag. I purposely positioned the galaxies against contrasting areas of the background felt for high visibility, but you can achieve more subtle effects by needlefelting similar colors instead.

Yarn:
Decadent Fibers Crème Puff, 20% mohair/79% Merino blend/1% nylon, 8 oz., 490 yd., Salsa (gold/orange/purple/fuchsia/rust variegated), 1 skein

Yarn Weight:
Bulky

Needles:
Size 15 (U.S.) circular, 16 in., or size 15 (U.S.) dpn, 12 in.
NOTE: If using a circular needle, you will also need an additional straight size 15 needle for the bind-off

Tools:
Large-eye blunt needle
Large-eye sharp needle

Notions:
Small bamboo handles
Small-gauge needlefelting needle 10-in. by 7-in. piece of foam, 4 in. thick
Matching sewing thread
1/8-in.-thick plywood, cut 9 3/4 in. long, 2 3/4 in. wide, with corners rounded (optional)

Unfelted Gauge:
2.5 sts = 1 in., 3 rnds = 1 in. in stockinette st

Number of Complete Washer Cycles to Felt as Shown:
(Adjust as necessary to achieve desired size.) Less than 1. Agitate 5–8 minutes, remove from washer, and rinse in lukewarm water.

Size before Felting:
Approx 14 in. long, 13 1/4 in. wide, lying flat

Size after Felting:
(NOTE: Sizes can vary due to individual washer cycles. Finished items that are too large can be felted again. Finished items that are too small can be stretched while wet to add about 15 percent additional length and/or width.) 8 in. long, 12 1/2 in. wide lying flat; 10 in. across, 7 in. tall, 3 in. wide at the bottom and sides after forming and pleating.

Number of Yarn Strands Used:
1 throughout
NOTE: The dye on this yarn bleeds a little. Do not felt with items knitted from any other yarn.

KNITTING INSTRUCTIONS

With Salsa and size 15 needles (dpn or 16 in. circular), CO 66 sts. Make sure the stitches aren't twisted, and join.

RND 1: K.

Work even until bag measures 14 in. Divide the sts evenly on 2 needles (or divide the sts in half on the circular needle, and slide the stitches toward the tips of the needles, leaving an empty loop at the center division). Turn the bag inside out. Work a 3-needle bind-off by binding off 1 st from each needle together across the bottom of the bag. Tie off the remaining loop, and cut a 1-in. tail.

With the bag still inside out, flatten one corner so that the bottom seam is centered. With yarn threaded in a large-eye needle, sew across the corner, 2 in. from the end, as indicated (see p. 154). Repeat with the other bottom corner. Turn the bag right side out and felt, and then trim the corners as directed.

FELTING

Place bag in a mesh zippered lingerie bag and wash on the hot/cold cycle. Check the progress frequently and remove the bag when the desired amount of felting has taken place. Rinse in lukewarm water and spin to remove excess moisture. Trim the excess fabric from the sewn corner triangles, close to the seam. Pull the bag into shape, making upper edges straight, flattening the bottom, and creasing the pleats in the sides. Allow bag to dry.

NEEDLEFELTING INSTRUCTIONS

NOTE: Needlefelting needles are barbed and very sharp. Use caution when needlefelting.

1. Decide which side of the bag is to be the front. Place the 4-in.-thick foam piece inside the bag.
2. Select an approximately 12-in. length of unfelted yarn and, starting in an area where the color of the yarn contrasts with the color of the felted bag, anchor the yarn by poking several times with the needlefelting needle, using an upright stabbing motion.
3. Continue to wind the yarn around the original anchor, in a close spiral, poking the yarn with the needlefelting needle at regular intervals, until you have wound all of the yarn, or the circle is the size you wish it to be. If you don't like the design or placement of the spiral, pull it out, reform the shape, and anchor it again. You can add more yarn if you want, in any color you like.
4. Use the needlefelting needle to poke the yarn throughout the entire circle of wound yarn. This may take several hundred jabs. The spiral is firmly embedded when the yarn is uniformly tight and even (it will be stuck to the foam on the inside of the bag). If portions of the yarn still look loose and unformed, continue jabbing. If you "over-poke" the yarn and the line looks faint or disappears entirely, simply cut a small piece of yarn and needlefelt that over the original line.

5. Continue adding circles where and as you desire, making sure that the color of the outermost spiral contrasts with the felted bag color. (The bag shown here has 8 needlefelted circles distributed evenly on the front of the bag.) Carefully remove the foam after you finish needlefelting the yarn circles. You may want to experiment with a few half-circles that move off the "edge" of the purse to vary the pattern.

FINISHING

1. With matching sewing thread, tack the crease of each corner at the upper edge of the purse to help retain the side shaping.
2. With matching yarn in a large-eye needle, sew the bamboo handles centered on the front and back upper edge of the bag.
3. If desired, place the ⅛-in. plywood piece in the bottom of the bag to hold the shape while in use.

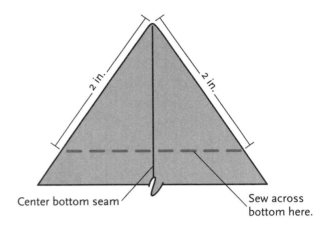

2 in. 2 in.

Center bottom seam

Sew across bottom here.

COSMOS BAG CORNER SEAM

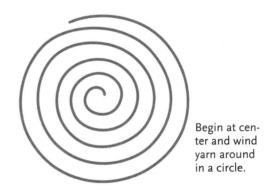

Begin at center and wind yarn around in a circle.

COSMOS BAG NEEDLEFELTING GUIDE

needlefelted folk art
santa ornaments

Get ready for the holidays when you knit and felt

these adorable primitive Santas, then needlefelt the details with yarn, unspun wool, or mohair locks. This simple pattern can be adjusted easily to make thinner, fatter, taller, or shorter Santas or other holiday sprites. Improvise a tree full of these cheery fellows, or tie one on every holiday package.

Yarn:
Knit Picks Wool of the Andes, 100% Peruvian wool, 50 g, 110 yd., #23765 Iron Ore and #23774 Chocolate, 1 skein each Knit Picks Bare—Peruvian Wool Worsted Weight, 100% Peruvian wool, 100 g, 220 yd., #23417 Natural, 1 skein

Yarn Weight:
Worsted

Needles:
Size 9 (U.S.) straight, 10 in.

Tools:
Large-eye blunt needle
Large-eye sharp needle
Fine-gauge needlefelting needles

Sturdy foam, at least 2 in. thick and 8 in. square

Notions:
For Fleece Santas: small amounts of peach, red, black, and white unspun wool, or white mohair locks; for Yarn Santas: small amounts of peach wool yarn DMC #5284 metallic gold embroidery floss, 8 in. for each Santa

Unfelted Gauge:
4.5 sts = 1 in., 6 rows = 1 in. in stockinette st

Number of Complete Washer Cycles to Felt as Shown:
(Adjust as necessary to achieve desired size.) 2

Sizes before Felting:
Narrow Santa: 8½ in. long, 5 in. wide; Wide Santa: 8 in. long, 6¾ in. wide

Sizes after Felting:
(NOTE: Sizes can vary due to individual washer cycles. Finished items that are too large can be felted again. Finished items that are too small can be stretched while wet to add about 15 percent additional length and/or width.)
Narrow Santa: 6 in. long, 3½ in. wide; Wide Santa: 5¼ in. long, 4½ in. wide

Number of Yarn Strands Used:
1 throughout

KNITTING INSTRUCTIONS

Wide Santa

With size 9 needles and Chocolate, CO 10.

Work in stockinette st for 2 in. End with a purl row.

BODY ROW 1: Cut Chocolate. Tie on Iron Ore. K across. CO 10 sts.

BODY ROW 2: P across. CO 10 sts. (30 sts)

BODY ROWS 3–4: Work even in stockinette st.

BODY DECREASE ROW 1: K2 tog, K across.

BODY DECREASE ROW 2: P2 tog, P across.

Repeat Body Decrease Rows 1–2 until 15 sts remain.

HAIR ROW 1: Cut Iron Ore. Tie on Natural. Continue decreasing as before until 8 sts remain.

NEXT ROW: Cut Natural. Tie on Iron Ore. Continue decreasing as before until 1 st remains.

Cut yarn, thread through last loop, and tighten. Weave loose ends in along the edge.

WIDE SANTA VARIATION: Work as above, cutting Iron Ore and tying Natural when 18 sts remain. Work with Natural until 10 sts remain. Cut Natural and tie on Iron Ore. Finish as above.

Narrow Santa

With size 9 needles and Chocolate, CO 8.

Work in stockinette st for 2½ in. End with a purl row.

BODY ROW 1: Cut Chocolate. Tie on Iron Ore. K across, CO 7.

BODY ROW 2: P across, CO 7. (22 sts)

BODY ROWS 3–4: Work even in stockinette st.

BODY DECREASE ROW 1: Dec 1 st at the beg and end of row.

BODY DECREASE ROWS 2–3: Work in stockinette st. Repeat Body Decrease Rows 1–3 until 12 sts remain.

HAIR ROW 1: Cut Iron Ore. Tie on Natural. Work as before until 8 sts remain.

NEXT ROW: Tie on Iron Ore, and continue working until 2 sts remain. Cut yarn and pull through remaining loops. Weave in loose ends along the edges.

NARROW SANTA VARIATION: Work as above, cutting Iron Ore and tying on Natural when 16 sts remain. Work until 12 sts remain. Cut Natural and tie on Iron Ore. Finish as above.

FELTING

Place Santas in a mesh zippered lingerie bag and wash on the hot/cold cycle. Check the progress frequently and remove them when the desired amount of felting has taken place. Remove the Santas from the lingerie bag and pull them into shape, making edges straight and flattening the piece. Allow the Santas to dry.

> **YOU CAN VARY THE WIDTH OF YOUR SANTA** easily by casting on more red suit stitches. You can vary the height of your Santa easily by working more brown boot rows. You can vary the placement of the face and hair by working the natural rows either earlier or later than indicated in the pattern instructions.

NEEDLEFELTING INSTRUCTIONS

NOTE: Needlefelting needles are barbed and very sharp. Use caution when needlefelting.

Fleece Needlefelted Santas

1. Lay the felted and dried Santa on the needlefelting foam.
2. Following the Fleece Needlefelting Guide, place a small amount of peach fleece on the white section, as shown in Step 1. Using a fine-gauge needlefelting needle, poke through the fleece and the felted Santa with an upright stabbing motion. Repeat every ⅛ in. around the outside edge of the peach fleece. If you

want a bigger face for your Santa, add more peach wool. If you want a smaller face, carefully pull the fleece away from the Santa.

3. Once you are happy with the size and shape of the face, poke the peach circle repeatedly around the outer edge and all through the center. Work evenly on the whole circle, always keeping the needle at a

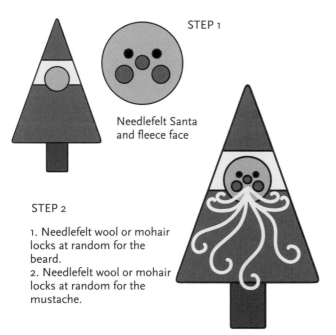

STEP 1

Needlefelt Santa and fleece face

STEP 2

1. Needlefelt wool or mohair locks at random for the beard.
2. Needlefelt wool or mohair locks at random for the mustache.

FLEECE NEEDLEFELTING GUIDE

STEP 1

Needlefelt Santa and yarn face

STEP 2

1. Tie lengths for the mustache and beard in the middle.
2. Needlefelt the beard in place.
3. Needlefelt the mustache in place.

YARN NEEDLEFELTING GUIDE

90-degree angle to the foam. The face is anchored fully when the circle looks embossed. The Santa will be embedded in the foam at this stage.

4. When you are happy with the face, place small bits of red unspun wool as shown in Step 2 for the cheeks and nose. Anchor and needlefelt as for the face.

5. If you are using mohair locks for the beard, select 4 or 5 and place them on the body as shown in Step 2 (remember that you can use as many as you like, and place the locks wherever you want). Anchor the locks in place along the length of each one. When you are happy with the number of locks and the placement of the beard, go back and embed the locks fully. You may leave the curly ends un-needlefelted.

6. Center one mohair lock directly under the nose for the mustache. Anchor the lock in place as shown, and then embed it fully.

7. If you are using unspun wool or wool locks, anchor and place as for the mohair locks.

8. Carefully loosen the Santa from the foam. The needle-felted fibers will extend through to the back of the Santa.

Yarn Needlefelted Santas

1. Place the Santa on the foam. Cut an 8-in. piece of peach wool yarn, form in a close spiral on the Santa as shown in Step 1 of the Yarn Needlefelting Guide, and anchor it in place. When you are happy with the size and shape of the face, needlefelt as above, working along the entire spiral of yarn. If there are open or empty spots in the face, fill them in with short lengths of peach yarn.

2. When the face is needlefelted to your satisfaction, place small spirals of Iron Ore yarn for the cheeks and nose, and needlefelt in place as shown in Step 2.

3. Place small spirals of Chocolate yarn for the eyes, and needlefelt in place.

4. Cut 3 6-in. pieces of Natural yarn, and tie them together in the center with a 4-in. length of Natural yarn. Place the tie below the nose and anchor in place. Arrange the yarn for the beard as you like, and anchor the curlicues in place. You may add more strands if you like. When you are satisfied with the placement of the beard strands, needlefelt along the length of each strand.

5. Cut 2 4-in. pieces of Natural yarn, and tie them together in the center with a 4-in. length of Natural yarn. Place the tie just below the nose and anchor in place. Arrange and anchor the mustache strands as you like. When you are satisfied with the placement of the mustache strands, needlefelt along the length of each strand.

6. If desired, needlefelt a length of Natural yarn above the eyes as a hat brim.

7. Carefully remove the Santa from the foam.

FINISHING

Thread an 8-in. length of metallic gold embroidery floss in a large-eye sharp needle. Sew through the top point of Santa's hat and tie the floss in a loop for a hanger.

knitting TERMS & ABBREVIATIONS

✳ Work the stitch directions within the asterisks (*...*) as many times as the directions instruct

beg Beginning

BO Bind-off

bobble A raised texture stitch worked by increasing and decreasing stitches in a defined area

cable Place the directed number of stitches on a cable needle and hold in front or behind the work, knit the directed number of stitches from the left needle, place the cable needle stitches on the left needle and work them as directed.

cable needle A short, double-pointed needle used to hold cable stitches

circular Knitting needles connected with a flexible cable that can be used for knitting flat (back and forth) or in the round.

CO Cast on

cont Continue

dec Decrease, usually by knitting two stitches together, or PSSO

dpn(s) Double-pointed needles—the stitches are divided evenly on three or four needles, and the work is knitted in the round.

Fair Isle A colorwork technique using no more than two colors in any single row, where unused colors are stranded loosely on the wrong side of the work. Usually worked in the round.

felt Knitted wool fabric purposely shrunk with water, soap, and agitation to form a thick, fuzzy fabric

felting The process of using water, soap, and agitation to create a thick, fuzzy fabric

flat Knitting that is worked back and forth, usually on straight needles

foam Thick upholstery-style foam placed inside/underneath items to be needlefelted, to provide support

fulled Another term for knitted wool fabric purposely shrunk with water, soap, and agitation to create a thick, fuzzy fabric

g Grams

I-cord A technique for making a round knitted cord, using two dpns

inc Increase, usually by picking up a strand from the row below and knitting it (see Pick Up and Knit)

intarsia A colorwork technique where color changes are made by tying on new yarn colors and following a chart. Extra colors are not stranded across the back of the work. Usually worked flat (back and forth).

in the round A technique where stitches are either placed on double-pointed needles or on a circular needle. The stitches are joined and the knitting proceeds around the piece, always on the right side.

K Knit

LT Left twist—a cable stitch where the twist travels to the left

needlefelt(ing) The process of anchoring wool yarn or unspun wool fleece to a felted piece using a barbed needle to enmesh the fibers

needlefelting needle The barbed needle used to enmesh wool yarn or unspun fleece to a felted background

P Purl

patt Pattern

pick up and knit A method of increasing the number of stitches by picking up a strand from the row below, and knitting it. (see Increase)

PSSO Pass the slipped stitch over the knit stitch—a method of decreasing (see Decrease)

rnd Round—a row worked with the stitches joined. All work is knitted on the right side of the piece.

row A row worked flat (back and forth)

RS Right side, the front of the work

RT Right twist—a cable stitch where the twist travels to the right

Sl Slip the stitch to the right needle, as if to purl; do not knit the stitch

st(s) Stitch(es)

Tail The length of yarn left after tying on, or cutting yarn

three-needle bind-off A method of binding off stitches that seams two pieces of knitting together

tighten and tie off After the tail is pulled through the remaining stitches (see Weave Through), pull the tail tight to close the opening in the stitches. Sew a small knot so that the tail does not loosen.

tog Together

turn Turn the knitting and work on the other side. Usually at the end of a row, but also in the middle of the row, as indicated, when turning a heel.

weave ends in Thread the tail in a large-eye blunt needle, and draw the needle through several loops on the wrong side of the piece. Trim the tail flush with the fabric.

weave through Thread the tail in a large-eye blunt needle, and draw the needle through the remaining stitches left on the needle(s). Tighten and tie off the yarn, and weave the end in on the wrong side of the piece.

U.S. United States knitting needle sizes

WS Wrong side, the back of the work

yd Yard

resources

yarns

Brown Sheep Company, Inc
www.brownsheep.com

Decadent Fibers
Also suppliers of needlefelting wool
www.decadentfibers.com

Cascade Yarns
www.cascadeyarns.com

Crystal Palace Yarns
www.straw.com/cpy/

Knit Picks Yarns
Craftsamericana Group, Inc.
www.knitpicks.com

Noro Yarns
Distributed in the U.S. by Knitting Fever
www.knittingfever.com

notions

BEADS
Mainstay Crafts
Manufactured by Sulyn Industires
www.sulyn.com

PAINT
DecoArt Crafters Acrylic
www.decoart.com

MAGNETIC CLOSURES
Clover
www.clover-usa.com

SEQUINS
Cartwright's Sequins
www.ccartwright.com

TOOLS
Needlefelting Tools
FeltCrafts
www.feltcrafts.com

index

Note: **Bold** page numbers indicate that an illustration or photo appears, and *italicized* page numbers indicate a table. (When only one number of a page range is **bold** or *italicized*, illustrations or tables appear on one or more of the pages.)